This particular topic, the development of w⟨ ... ⟩eaders, could not have been written at a more appropriate time. At a time when the world is experiencing a major economic crisis and we have to fundamentally rethink the topic of economics and the corporate world, it is vitally important to talk about the inclusion of women in senior leadership roles, and develop the kind of women leaders who could develop an economic system with a conscience.

Mardia van der Walt, Senior Vice President and Regional Head Africa & Middle East, Chairman of the Board, T-Systems South Africa

Dr. Kelan's thoughtful and careful examination of how women in their twenties and thirties can be positioned as leaders is a timely and needed piece of research. Since slightly more than 25% of the world population is classified as Millennial's and the issue of gender equity remains a global issue, understanding this intersection is critical for all of us.

Todd Corley, Senior Vice President and Global Chief Diversity Officer, Abercrombie & Fitch

A great book that addresses real issues facing our youth, particularly in our region ... A lot to learn from highlighting the important leadership role women can play in our part of the world.

Nabil Habayeb, President and CEO, GE Middle East, North Africa & Turkey

Through an organization's deliberate and strategic focus on the six elements discussed in Elisabeth Kelan's book, boardrooms will start to look very different as this female generation starts to show what leadership of the future looks like and what business impact can be made.

Caroline Barth, HR VP, Novartis Canada

'Dr. Elisabeth Kelan is my source of inspiration.'
Maria Kristiina Ståhl, Staff Committee Deputy Spokesperson, European Central Bank

Expanding the numbers of women in leadership positions through lessons learned and best practices is necessary to bring gender equality to scale in business, and in other arenas as well. Only then will we realize the business case benefits that extend throughout a company and beyond to communities, especially through the supply chain.
Joan Libby Hawk, Special Advisor, UN Women's and UN Global Compact's Partnership Initiative: Women's Empowerment Principles

Elisabeth Kelan is a bright light in the field of gender and diversity and inclusion research. Her work is important for companies, universities, and individuals.
Tanya M Odom Ed.M., Global Consultant and Executive Coach

An innovative perspective at the intersection of the main influences shaping the way work works in the 21st century: the female factor and the Millennials.
Aniela Unguresan, Co-Founder

RISING STARS

Developing Millennial Women as Leaders

Elisabeth Kelan, PhD

palgrave
macmillan

First published 2012 by
PALGRAVE MACMILLAN

Palgrave Macmillan in the UK is an imprint of Macmillan Publishers Limited,
registered in England, company number 785998, of Houndmills, Basingstoke,
Hampshire RG21 6XS.

Palgrave Macmillan in the US is a division of St Martin's Press LLC,
175 Fifth Avenue, New York, NY 10010.

Palgrave Macmillan is the global academic imprint of the above companies
and has companies and representatives throughout the world.

Palgrave® and Macmillan® are registered trademarks in the United States,
the United Kingdom, Europe and other countries.

ISBN 978–0–230–29401–1

This book is printed on paper suitable for recycling and made from fully
managed and sustained forest sources. Logging, pulping and manufacturing
processes are expected to conform to the environmental regulations of the
country of origin.

A catalogue record for this book is available from the British Library.

A catalog record for this book is available from the Library of Congress.

10   9   8   7   6   5   4   3   2   1
21 20 19 18 17 16 15 14 13 12

Printed and bound in Great Britain by
CPI Antony Rowe, Chippenham and Eastbourne

To my grandmothers
Christa Wehrmann
and
Nevin Keçecioğlu

CONTENTS

CONTENTS

CONTENTS

LIST OF FIGURES AND TABLE

Figures

Table

FOREWORD

As the UK Chairman and Senior Partner of the UK's largest professional services firm, I have the opportunity to meet with senior business leaders on a daily basis. One common topic in these conversations is the challenge of attracting, developing and retaining leaders who reflect the increasingly diverse nature of the modern workforce. Increasingly the business leaders I am talking to see this not simply as a question of 'doing the right thing', but more fundamentally as being essential for the growth of their business.

None of us should underestimate the challenge. In a PwC survey published in December 2011 'Millennials at Work: Shaping the Workplace' we found that only 18% of Millennials said they intended to stay with their current employer. And in the PwC 15th Annual Global CEO Survey launched at Davos in January 2012 we reported how CEOs around the world had told us talent shortages and mismatches were impacting business profitability. One in four CEOs said they were unable to pursue a market opportunity or have had to cancel or delay a strategic initiative because of a shortage of talent.

So what does all this mean for business? The old ways of doing things need to change. PwC employs around 165,000 people globally, 50% of whom are women and 40% Millennials or Generation Y. We recruit a rich diversity of talent from schools and universities. But we need to ensure this diversity of talent is better reflected at the more senior levels of the organization. To achieve this we know we need to change some pretty fundamental things, such as long-established ways of working and commonly held stereotypical perceptions, particularly those relating to gender. These things take time which is why I believe diversity needs to be addressed as a change management programme – changing mindsets and behaviours.

There is no 'silver bullet' when it comes to diversity of talent but we do know from our own experience that many of the things we need to change to engage better with Generation Y (e.g. offering a greater variety of working arrangements) will benefit other groups, especially women.

A successful diversity strategy and plan requires engagement at three levels: the head, the heart and the hands. The business case for diversity (the head) addresses the first. Emotional engagement is what's required (the heart) if people are to act but the question often asked is 'What actions are needed?' Practical guidance (the hands) is essential.

The framework presented in this book is well researched and, based on our own experience at PwC, it captures the key areas of focus for developing Millennial women. These include the need for role models and authenticity, visibility, networking and organizational culture. It is above all practical.

To grow sustainable businesses, we need to ensure that those entering the workforce today are developed into leaders who are fit to lead into the future. This means creating the right conditions within our workplaces which successfully attract, develop and retain young talent and so help grow the pipeline of women leaders. This book is an important contribution to that process.

Ian Powell
UK Chairman and Senior Partner
PwC

ACKNOWLEDGEMENTS

I am writing this acknowledgement while overlooking the ruins of the old castle in Staufen in the Black Forest region of Germany. Staufen is a town mainly known for being the location of one of the most celebrated pieces of German literature: *Faust* by Johann Wolfgang Goethe. The protagonist, Dr Faust, is a scholar who is hungry to acquire knowledge. His quest to acquire knowledge makes him restless and unable to enjoy life. In modern day terminology we would talk about 'work–life conflict' and 'burn out'. The literary solution to this dilemma was for Dr Faust to make a pact with the devil, which transforms him into a young man who travels the world and lives through various adventures (apologies to my former German teacher Dr Demmer for shortening the storyline so inadequately).

The restlessness of today's academics is more driven by the demands of teaching routines, administrative responsibilities and journal publication pressures. I am therefore grateful for the fact that King's College London afforded me a relief from teaching and administrative duties, which I used to work on this book. The restlessness of modern academic life also means that I am very grateful for the patience that the editorial staff at Palgrave Macmillan has shown with the book – moving the deadline not only once but twice! In particular, I would like to thank my editors Eleanor Davey-Corrigan and Stephen Rutt, as well as Hannah Fox, for their valuable input.

Like the travels of Dr Faust, this manuscript travelled the world with me. It was written during research visits at the University of St. Gallen as well as Georgetown University and I would like to thank my hosts Dr Julia Nentwich and Dr Christopher Metzler for their kind invitations. Parts of the book were also written on the top floor of an hotel on the Palm Island in Dubai, in a charming hotel room in Paris, in a quaint small house in the centre of Funchal on Madeira, in wonderful apartments and coffee shops just south of Central Park and on the Upper East Side in New York City (thanks to

Christa Dowling and Elaine Papas for hosting me!) as well as in my family's home in Freiburg in the Black Forest. And of course, much of the book has been written in London.

This book has also profited immensely from the close collaboration with Dale Meikle and Sarah Churchman from PwC. I thank them for the countless insightful conversations and the wonderful support they provided throughout the process of writing this book. I admire their creative and change-provoking work at PwC immensely and they both continue to be an inspiration to me. I also would like to thank Rachel Dunkley Jones for her constructive feedback on an earlier draft of the book and for being such a resourceful research assistant during the early stages of the project. Dr Alice Mah helped me to collect much of the material and has helped me to think through many issues raised in this book. Dr Michael Lehnert not only supported me during the highs and lows of writing this book but also assisted me with various aspects of the research. Rachael Lemon created the wonderful illustration of the heuristic – thanks for that. I also would like to thank Karin Kohlberg for being so patient in taking pictures of me for this book in her lovely loft in New York City where she normally welcomes high-profile stars and not camera-shy academics.

While Dr Faust wanted to experience everything himself, I relied to a large degree on individuals sharing their experiences with me. The research would not have been possible without the individuals telling me their stories either formally or informally. I would also like to acknowledge the kind support of PwC (UK and Germany), American Express, Aviva, Baxter International, Cassidian, General Electric and Thomson Reuters for working with me on the signature practices. The research is based on the work done for a consortium on Generation Y convened by the Lehman Brothers Centre for Women in Business at London Business School. The consortium included the following partner companies: Accenture (founding partner), Allen & Overy, Barclaycard Business, Baxter International, Cargill, IBM, Johnson & Johnson and KPMG. I would like to thank London Business School for helping to provide such a fruitful environment for part of the research. Professor Lynda Gratton mentored me at London Business School and provided a lot of advice on how to shape and present research. Professor Judy Wajcman was a great sounding board for our research ideas and never tired of providing us with advice. Ellen Miller with her wealth of experience ensured that the research was relevant to practitioners. Lamia Walker did an excellent job managing the relationships with the corporate sponsors. Katharine Buckley and Enid Silverstone ensured not only a smooth running of the Centre but also provided a lot of input into the research.

I also profited from many academic discussions with my colleagues and friends and I would particularly like to thank Professor Rosalind Gill, Professor Silvia Gherardi, Professor Mustafa Özbilgin, Dr Sylvia Ann Hewlett, Dr Julia Nentwich and Tanya Odom for insightful discussions on this research. I presented the research in various forms and settings and would like to thank the engaged audiences for their feedback, too.

Some of the material covered in this book has been published in academic journals with the publishers Academy of Management, Emerald and Wiley Blackwell:

- Kelan, E. K. and Dunkley Jones, R. (2009) 'Reinventing the MBA as a Rite of Passage for a Boundaryless Era'. *Career Development International*, 14(6): 547–69.
- Kelan, E. K. and Dunkley Jones, R. (2010) 'Gender and the MBA'. *Academy of Management Learning & Education*, 9(1): 26–43.
- Kelan, E. K. and Mah, A. (Online Early) 'Gendered Identification: Between Idealization and Admiration'. *British Journal of Management*, http://onlinelibrary.wiley.com/doi/10.1111/j.1467-8551.2012.00834.x

I would also like to acknowledge the reuse of one table, which appeared in a different publication by the Pew Research Center before:

- Zickuhr, K. (2010) 'Generations 2010', Pew Internet & American Life Project: Table 1, A US Perspective on Generations, http://www.pewinternet.org/~/media//Files/Reports/2010/PIP_Generations_and_Tech10.pdf (p. 4).

I thank Shiva Rea and her global Prana Flow® community for allowing me to rejuvenate, revitalize and relax from the long hours of typing and editing. As always I am deeply grateful to my family for their moral support.

1

INTRODUCTION

INTRODUCTION

Leonora is sitting opposite her career coach. She has decided to seek advise because she feels at crossroads in her career and her life. At 26 she is part of the generation that is commonly called Millennials. She had done particularly well to secure her dream job in a consultancy at a time when many were being laid off. The first few months had been exciting for her but now after four years, she was bored with the job. It could no longer excite her. She travelled a lot, which she had always wanted to do, but just seeing client sites was not really comparable to traveling for leisure. She had great colleagues and enjoyed meeting them outside work too, but apart from that she had few friends. While she was not very unhappy with her work and life, she somehow felt that she was not on the right track. She had contemplated about visiting a career coach for some time and was finally meeting one in her practice.

After listening to the reasons why Leonora wanted to see her, her career coach asked her what her plans in life were. Leonora did not know. This was in part why she wanted to talk to the career coach. She felt that she could not be herself at work but had to pretend to be someone else to fit into the organization. Her career coach asks if there is anyone at work or in her social network whom she admires and would like to emulate. For Leonora that was exactly the problem. She had noticed that there were few senior women around and those that she knew of were, in Leonora's view, living lives that she would not like to live. These women worked all the hours and did not have children, and if they had children they never saw them. Leonora also felt that they were not supporting her. At a networking event, the senior women really did not appear interested in Leonora as a person. The only thing she knew was that she did not want to be like any of those women but this seemed to be the only acceptable model in her organization.

The career coach wanted to know what Leonora wanted from work. Leonora paused and thought. She replied that she wanted to keep learning new things to improve herself. For this she felt that feedback was really important because it would help her to improve her performance. If she was at the top of her game, she would find work elsewhere, too. Learning was central to her. The career coach asked if she had thought about an MBA degree to add some formal training to her CV. Leonora stated that she had indeed thought about it and had looked at some business schools. She had also talked with some of her friends who did MBAs and they talked about the self-transforming experiences and the intense community they experienced. While Leonora thought that this was a great idea, she had also heard stories of her female friends of how they were not listened to in teamwork and how competitive the culture of the MBA degree was. That was less appealing to Leonora, who felt lucky because she never experienced any gender discrimination in her life before, apart from maybe being asked to bring coffee once but that was only because the client was very conservative.

Again the career coach asked what she wanted from work; Leonora replied that she wanted to work on exciting projects that would allow her to gain visibility in the organization. However she felt that her reputation was tarnished a bit because she had worked on a prestigious project that had gone totally wrong. Although she had very little impact on the overall running of the project, she noticed that after the project had failed she was not selected for some of the projects she would have loved to work on. What Leonora wanted was to have a manager who was a bit more like her career coach, who would talk issues through with her and help her develop. Instead she often felt like a dispensable resource that could be replaced at any minute. She had to work long hours to get her deliverables through and constant travel had left a toll on her health. She was tired and exhausted. The constant pressures at work made her feel like she was drifting along. This was not the life she had expected and the thought of working like this for the next 50 years depressed her.

Leonora's experience is not untypical for the Millennial generation. After some years in the labour market this generation of junior professionals seems dissatisfied with their career progress and drained of motivation. Managers of Millennials regularly lament the fact that this generation is spoiled and does not want to work hard. The focus on generation often means that gender is ignored. Gender will, however, play a role in how Millennials experience work and plan their careers. In this introductory chapter, I will outline the central area of interest for this book. This will mean defining what we mean by generation and gender as well as leadership. I will also offer an outline of this book.

THE INTERSECTIONALITY BETWEEN GENDER AND GENERATION

The topics of gender and generation are currently on the top of many corporate agendas. Millennials or people from Generation Y have been a popular topic in the general and business press. A cover story of *US Today* for instance claimed that Millennials are not as different as presumed earlier (Healy, 2012) and *Fox Business* claims that Generation Y is seeking work–life balance (Mielach, 2012). Even in aging workforces like the US, Millennials forms a fairly large generation in terms of size (Zickuhr, 2010). In emerging markets like China it is expected that 50% of the working age population belong to the Millennial generation (Lynton & Thogersen, 2010). This makes it important for organizations to find out what makes this generation tick. Women are often seen as an underused 'resource', too. In spite of decades of equal opportunities legislation in the Western world, women are still scarce in the most senior positions in organizations. This has led to heated debates about the merit of quotas and targets for women on boards and in senior roles. Very rarely are gender and generation considered together, but understanding how gender and generation work together might be able to provide answers to the questions of both why Millennials' views on work are different and why women are not making it to the top of organizations.

We colloquially often talk about generations without defining what a generation actually is. Academically, three facets of generational identities can be observed: the age-based definition, the cohort-based definition and the incumbency-based definition (Joshi et al., 2010). It is most common in practitioner research to use the age-based definition of generations. Generations are commonly divided into Silent Generation, Baby Boomers, Generation X and Generation Y/Millennials (see Table 1.1). Many approaches

Table 1.1 A US perspective on generations (modified from Zickuhr, 2010)

Name	Birth Years	Age in 2012	Percentage of US Population
Millennials	1977–92	20–35	30
Generation X	1965–76	36–47	19
Baby Boomers	1946–64	48–66	34
Silent & GI Generation	<1945	>67	16

to dividing generations are based on the work of Strauss and Howe's generational theory (Strauss & Howe, 1991), which is based on US history. This first of all means that in other regions of the world different factors might influence generations. In China the Millennial generation is shaped for instance by the One-child policy, which resulted in higher individualism than previous generations (Moore, 2005). In Strauss and Howe's (1991) generational theory the Millennial generation is born between 1982 and 2004. However there is considerable contestation in regard to when a specific generation starts and ends and in other academic research the Millennial generation would encompass birth years from 1977 to 1994 (Broadbridge, Maxwell & Ogden, 2007). There is also an obvious overlap between people born towards the outer perimeter of a generation who probably share more alike with the next generation than the start of their own generation. The generational definitions based on age should therefore be considered as having some overlap at the outer perimeters (see Figure 1.1).

Generations can also be understood as cohort-based generational identities. The focus is here on groups that experience events such as organizational entry at a similar time (Joshi et al., 2010). These are often used in research on organizational demography and would focus typically on shared socialization experiences. If a group of people enter an organization at about the same time they are prone to make similar experiences. Those similar experiences will lead to shared knowledge as well as strong bonds between those people.

Generations can also be understood as incumbency-based generational identities (Joshi et al., 2010). These perspectives are common in anthropology, where for instance it may be explored how kinship structures impact identity constructions. This means that how being a child, a parent or a grandparent has specific implications for the identity one can adopt. Such processes of identity formation can easily be transferred to business organizations where being a junior professional, a middle manager or a senior leader has clear implications for the type of identities that can be constructed. Being

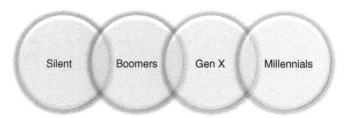

Figure 1.1 Overlapping generations

a junior professional will come with a certain set of expectations, which can be used as the basis for identity construction by either accepting or rejecting them. In addition, most junior professionals will not have started families. The identities are then transformed as the junior professional progresses through the ranks. This time also coincides with starting a family, which is often associated with a temporary withdrawal of women from the labour market. Senior professionals are confronted with yet another set of expectations they have to fulfil or reject. This perspective allows us to highlight that in each position in their life course individuals will meet certain expectations that have an impact on their identity formation.

In this book the focus will be on Millennials or individuals from Generation Y. Both terms are used simultaneously to describe this generation. I will also be drawing on all three facets of generational identity formation. In terms of the age group, I am focusing on individuals who were born between 1977 and 1987, which corresponds to the early tranche of the Millennial generation. Some of the informal interviews were also with people born in the early 1990s. This means that the older part of the Millennial generation is used here. In terms of cohorts-based identities, the main focus of the book are going to be people who either entered business school or who entered business organizations around the same time. This means that we are not focusing on all Millennials but a particular strata that has decided to enter a business career or business education. Their experiences are going to be different than other segments of the socio-economic strata (cf. Reeskens and van Oorschot, 2012). Finally, in regard to incumbency-based definitions, the subjects that feature in this book are mostly in junior ranks in organizations or are undergoing the transition from a junior person to a mid-level manager. Being a junior person in business without a family of their own often shapes the practices that these young professionals display. Using all three definitions of generational identities allows a move away from a narrow focus on just the year in which a person was born towards exploring what might have shaped their identities.

Having defined generations, let's turn to defining what we will understand by gender in this book. When one talks about gender in the workplace, most people understand that one talks about women. Gender is therefore often equated with women even though the definitions of gender include both women and men. The focus on women can be explained by the fact that women are indeed often the focus of attention when one talks about gender. Moreover it is women who are in the minority position in senior business roles, which might explain why gender research comes to be focused on women alone. Much research on women in business has for instance analysed the characteristics of the women who break the glass ceiling and issues around work–life balance that are said to hinder women to advance.

While this research is certainly important, the other side of gender, men, is often neglected. Yet as the majority in senior leadership roles they have a major impact on the organizational culture and on the mechanisms of inclusion and exclusion of women. Academic research on gender has therefore started to look at men in the work context, which is often talked about as masculinities (Cheng, 1996). In addition, it is often difficult to assess gender differences and similarities if only women are studied because a comparative group is missing. Leading research in the area acknowledges this and includes men as well as women in its research design (Wajcman, 1998) to explore potential similarities and differences along on gender lines.

Talking about gender is also markedly different from talking about 'sex' in the academic/biological sense. The sex/gender distinction was one of the hallmarks of the second wave of feminism. The distinction entails that sex is the biological make-up of men and women (female and male) whereas gender is the social construction of what is seen as the masculine and the feminine. More recent approaches to the sex/gender distinction have stressed that what we see as biological is also often socially constructed (Fausto-Sterling, 2000). By social construction it is meant that what we perceive as reality is actually the product of our own mind. While some people believe in unchanging essences of objects, social constructionism is interested in how people perceive (or construct) objects. In regard to gender, this would then mean exploring how people come to be perceived as masculine and feminine, and male and female.

Let's unpack this notion of the social construction of gender a bit further by looking at an example from my research. In my previous book *Performing Gender at Work*, I explored how gender is enacted in daily work situations and interviews (Kelan, 2009b). One of the most striking findings relates to the now celebrated social skills such as teamwork and relating to the customer. While social skills are required in a large variety of jobs, my research found that the new ideal worker in information communication technology (ICT) work not only needs technical knowledge but also social skills. However my research has indicated that it is men rather than women who continue to be seen as the ideal worker because social skills are seen as normal in women and are therefore not rewarded as special (Kelan, 2008b). In contrast, men who have social skills are perceived as unusual because they are perceived as acting against their natural inclination and are therefore seen as a particularly suitable ideal technology worker. Thereby the social construction of gender becomes evident in the fact that first of all skills were gendered but more importantly there were gendered differences in who was seen as most effective at performing the supposedly feminine skills.

In this book, I will adopt a social constructionist perspective of gender. This means first of all that a full-spectrum view of gender is offered. While the focus is on Millennial women, it is impossible to understand Millennial women without also understanding Millennial men. This will allow us to compare and contrast different perspectives with an awareness that there are not only differences between men and women but also among men and women. In other words, not all women will share the same perspectives neither will all men. Exploring differences among women and among men is important to fully explore the social construction of gender. In addition, gender will be seen as something that is performed, interacted with and done rather than just if a person is male and female. This will allow us to highlight the multitude of gender constructions that exist. In other words to understand Millennial women we need to understand their experiences in relation to Millennial men as well.

This book considers the *intersectionality* between gender and generations (Figure 1.2). What does intersectionality mean? Gender and generation can be understood as two dimensions of diversity. Intersectionality now means how these dimensions of diversity intersect and create set of challenges for the group affected (McCall, 2001). Intersectionality rose to the fore when analysis of Black women's experiences showed that they suffered a specific set of racial and gendered inequalities that could not be understood by only considering 'race'[1] or gender (Hill Collins, 2000). In a similar vein this

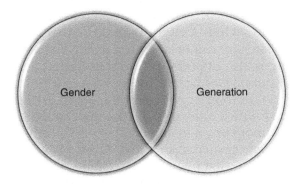

Figure 1.2 Intersectionality between gender and generation

book seeks to understand the specific challenges and opportunities raised by the intersections of gender and generation when seeking to understand Millennial women. It is thus argued that while we gain insight from looking at gender and generation individually, we will only fully comprehend Millennial women when we consider the intersectionality of gender and generation.

BUILDING THE HEURISTIC

There is a wealth of research on leadership development and how organizations and institutions can develop leaders. Leadership development is often seen as the development of high-potentials and a way to manage succession planning. While many practitioners would talk about talent when it comes to more junior professionals, I decided to talk about leadership development. This is the case because for junior professionals themselves being a potential leader was seen as more desirable than being considered as 'talent'. In the chapters that follow I develop a six-element heuristic with which to think through leadership development. A heuristic in the philosophical sense is an entity that is employed to understand another entity. It is basically a model for thinking through an issue. Here, I would like to begin by using the heuristic to think through the complexities of intersectionality.

The heuristic consists of six elements, which can subdivided into three categories (Figure 1.3). The three categories are self-knowledge, acquiring knowledge and social knowledge. Self-knowledge is linked here with role models and authenticity. *Role models* are used a place holder to describe the ability of individuals to explore potential versions of the self which in turn are central for what kind of leaders an individual can be (Ibarra, 2005). Second, it is often stressed that future leaders should be authentic (Avolio & Gardner, 2005; Goffee & Jones, 2005). *Authenticity* means being true to oneself and is often also expanded to include a responsibility to others.

The second category can be described as ways of acquiring knowledge. Training is also important for future leaders and can involve on-the-job or *experiential leading*. In this type of learning, feedback is crucially important to improving performance. Learning can also be formal learning, which often involves a status change such as moving from being a junior person in an organization to being a more senior person. This is encapsulated in the concept of the rite of passage (Van Gennep, 1960) that helps us understand status changes.

The final category can be summarized under social knowledge. In order to become a leader it is also vital to have *visibility*, which

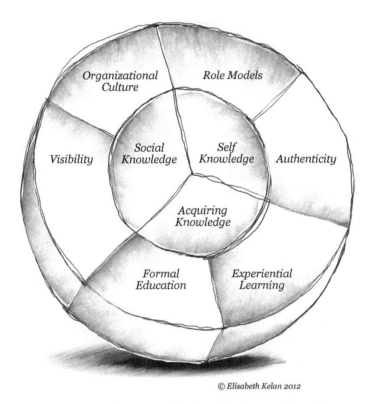

© Elisabeth Kelan 2012

Figure 1.3 The heuristic for developing Millennial women as leaders

means to have networks and to work on critical projects that develop a potential leader, allowing him or her to advance. Finally, the *organizational culture* needs to be receptive to developing future leaders. This means for instance being aware of potential stereotypes and having an organizational culture in which developing others is valued.

As outlined in the previous section intersectionality presumes that a specific set of challenges and opportunities emerges when the intersection of different dimensions of diversity, such as gender and generation, is considered. This is why in this case, the heuristic will first be used to explore gender, then generation and finally the intersection between gender and generations. Given that the interest here is on Millennial women, the focus will be on women and the Millennial generation.

Let's consider the heuristic from a gender perspective. In regard to self-knowledge, the lack of mentors, sponsors and *role models* is one of the most often quoted reasons why women are said not to succeed in businesses (Kilian, Hukai & McCarty, 2005; Ibarra,

Carter & Silva, 2010). Women are often discouraged from being *authentic* by practices and processes that prefer an incumbent-replacement mentality. As most incumbents of senior positions are men, women often try to emulate men to succeed. In regard to acquiring knowledge, it is often asserted that women need special *experiential learning* experiences to be trained as leaders. *Formal education* for management such as doing an MBA is still dominated by men. This means that women's experiences of doing an MBA will be impacted by being in a minority. For social knowledge, it is often argued that women have too much *visibility* as tokens but lack the right networks to move to senior positions. It is also often stated that the *organizational culture* in regard to work–life integration and stereotypical perceptions is preventing women from advancing.

Considering these elements from a Millennial perspective means the following. Let's start with self-knowledge. In regard to *role models* authenticity is key for Millennials. This *authenticity* is of course also of central importance when it comes to developing their own identities. *Experiential learning* is important for Millennials because it allows them to learn on the job and to develop their skills. Millennials will have many different careers in their lifespan because the jobs for life that previous generations were able to enjoy are withering away. In order to be able to have multiple careers throughout their lives, *formal education* is going to be a central element in acquiring the knowledge that allows Millennials to adapt their skills to fit the changing environment. In regard to social knowledge, networks are very important for Millennials to gain *visibility*. Research that we will discuss in the following has shown that Millennials have a desire for leisure time and this desire is larger than that of previous generations. This is why *organizational cultures* need to be able to adapt to Millennials' need to take work–life integration seriously.

If we want to consider intersectionality, we need to explore what the six elements mean for Millennial women. In regard to social knowledge, many Millennial women complain that they cannot find *role models*. *Authenticity* is also central for Millennial women yet they often find it difficult to achieve this authenticity in light of the demands of being both feminine and masculine so as to be perceived as leaders. Acquiring knowledge through *experiential learning* is a central way for Millennial women to learn and update their knowledge, and their experiences of *formal education* – such as doing an MBA – will be affected by being in a minority. Finally, social knowledge means that Millennial women need to create *visibility* through networks, but traditional women's networks are often not attractive to Millennial women. Millennial women also often find themselves in an organizational culture that does not embrace different modes of working and the tenets of diversity and inclusion.

The heuristic therefore allows us to think through the intersectionality of gender and generation as embodied in Millennial women in a multifaceted way. By using this heuristic, it is possible to develop processes and practices that are aware of generational and gender differences and similarities which will ensure that high potentials of today are developed into leaders that are fit to lead into the future. It will also ensure that the pipeline for women leaders is increased and that the potential that Millennials bring to the workplace is used to reshape working practices that are fit for the twenty-first century. However it is important to remember that heuristics are artificially held constant to explore the different dimensions based on the current state-of-the-art. This also means that as new insights become available the heuristic needs to be modified in a dynamic way to reflect the changing world of work.

THE RESEARCH EVIDENCE

It will be no surprise to the reader that this book is based on academic theories and research. Throughout the book as I develop the heuristic to think through how Millennial women can be developed as leaders, I will draw on academic literature. This focus does not mean that I do not value the practitioner research and the countless media articles that have been written on women, Millennials and Millennial women. In fact, I am an avid reader of this literature and I have gained much insight through it. For this book however I felt that what is missing is an appreciation of the academic insight that exists on gender and generations. As an academic, I felt I was in a unique position to offer my interpretation of this research and to bring it together with research I have done. Academic writing is often not easily accessible both due to a highly codified language and the fact that many academic journal articles have to be purchased at a fairly high cost by people who do not have access to university libraries (real and virtual). There is a lot of academic research available that is often only read by a small number of academics. Given how much work goes into academic journal articles and the unique insight they develop, it is important to share this knowledge with a wider public.

This book is based on five years of academic research and countless presentations and discussions with practitioners engaged in this topic. The research can best be described as falling into the *double hermeneutics* paradigm discussed by Anthony Giddens (1987).

Double hermeneutics describes the relationship between academic theories in the social sciences and practitioner or 'lay' understanding. Giddens distinguishes the social sciences from the natural sciences. In the natural sciences the researcher tries to uncover truths about the material world through controlled experiments. This way of understanding is one-way because the matter under study rarely talks back. However in the social sciences the situation is different: social scientists might study the behaviour of people and the findings of the study will have an impact on people that are studied. To put it in different words, after reading for instance a research report an individual might make the choice to act differently than described in the study. *Double hermeneutics* then means that practice shapes academic theories and those academic theories in turn shape practice. Given this mutual influence of theories and practice, this book attempts to carefully describe the academic evidence and see it through the lens of those who care about those issues and how they make sense about it. The book therefore not only includes the academic side of the story but also how the content is received by the audience and how it might impact behaviour. Moreover I actively seek to analyse this process of theory–practice interaction itself by seeing the reception as much as part of the research design rather than purely the academic data collection.

Most of the material I am going to cover is distinctly qualitative in nature. Quantitative research provides an overview of an area by surveying a great number of people and analysing their standardized answers using statistical software packages. Qualitative research in contrast goes into much more depth. It is not common to give interviewees closed standardized questions. Instead the skilled interviewer will guide the interviewee through a series of topics that are discussed in depth. While the topics and sample questions are fixed in advance in an interview guide, the interviewer has the liberty to probe deeper into certain aspects or to jump a section if the questions have been answered before. The interviewer is determined to establish a trusting relationship to the interviewee in which the interviewee feels safe to express their opinions without fear of any negative repercussions. Skilled interviewers are trained to listen and use similar words to the interviewees in their questions. The interviewer has to be socially competent to read the interviewee. Conducting an in-depth interview that goes beyond a superficial conversation is a real craft and art. The interviewers I worked with on this project all have several years of Ph.D. training in qualitative research under their belt.

In order to protect the identities of those who shared their thoughts with us, I follow normal academic practice and use pseudonyms for individuals and do not disclose the organizations in which they individuals worked. None of the names are real and I have disguised certain elements of the story to protect this anonymity. In some cases, this involves taking inspiration from real persons but creating fictitious personas for the purpose of illustrating certain points. Most of the people you will meet when I discuss the empirical research evidence are based on actual interview transcripts with some disguising elements where required. For the examples I use to open the chapters I provide fuller profiles of people and use more liberty in telling their stories. The persona I used to open this book is however a composite of different stories that were collected as part of the research. This person is there to guide us through the heuristic which is developed and illustrate the real life impact.

It is also common practice in qualitative research to quote interviewees extensively when one presents research evidence. I have consciously departed from this norm and have decided to narrate the interview extracts. Academically such a move would be seen as controversial and you will be able to see in many of my publications that I do carefully cite and analyse interview extracts. I have decided not do this in this book, because I wanted to describe the people we interviewed and their perspectives in a fuller way than would be allowed by traditional interview extracts. You will still get a flavour of what people originally said but you will read them through my narrative. Through this I not only hope to do their contribution more justice but also to make myself more visible in the research. What these people told me and my colleagues was in response to questions we asked and it is important to be aware of this dynamic, which academics call reflexivity.

The seed for this book was the research project on Generation Y that we conducted at the Centre for Women in Business at London Business School. This research entailed detailed interviews with young professionals. Those young professionals were born between 1977 and 1987 and had either joined a graduate training programme in one of two blue chip companies or they were studying for an MBA degree. We conducted 52 formal interviews with some follow up interviews. Our sample was truly international, and included people who came originally from all five continents. They of course shared the fact that they had all came to work in the global metropolis of London. They thereby belong to the globally mobile elite of highly-educated individuals who come to London in to establish themselves professionally and in search of new and exciting experiences. Not only was this group very international, it was also diverse. We ensured that we interviewed men and women in equal numbers and sampled individuals with different abilities, different sexual orientations and different ethnic and religious backgrounds.

If one is only used to quantitative research, one might easily say that such a sample is too small and too unrepresentative to say anything meaningful at all about the world. Academically qualitative research is well established and we used the normal 'safeguards' to ensure that the research is methodologically sound. This for instance includes using expert interviewers who are able to go really deeply into what people think. To help this process we drew a lot on pictures and images which helped explore in depth the meaning-making processes of individuals. In qualitative research the analysis takes a long time and includes a word-by-word transcription of the interviews. These transcripts are then read several times and entered into a computer programme that assists with coding. Coding is the process of putting similar segments from different talks together. Those codes were then analysed based on what they share and how they are different. Through this processes the meaning is carefully unfolded. This meaning is often contradictory. Interactions between human beings are littered with contradictions and we might say something that contradicts what we say five seconds, minutes or hours later. In qualitative research those contradictions are carefully analysed because they show us a lot about how meaning is made and which function it serves in a context.

After analysing the material, we wrote up a report entitled 'The Reflexive Generation – Young Professionals' Perspectives on Work, Career and Gender' (Kelan et al., 2009). In this report we outlined some of the early findings. We presented the results to a group of practitioners and had a roundtable discussion to see what they made of the results. Consequently I have presented the research results to various audiences worldwide. I engaged a lot with practitioners from major companies and international organizations to get their feedback. In addition, I spoke to many women's groups and networks on these issues and was particularly pleased that many younger women joined the discussion and shared their views. These discussions helped a lot to refine the theories we developed and to make them more relevant to practice. I was able to add many new points of view that were not present in the research, which made it much richer.

In addition, I had the pleasure of teaching students at different universities over the last years and I presented my research on the topic whenever I could. This has helped immensely to make sense of the material and to pick up on new elements that I had not considered before. Having many students born in the 1990s, and so a bit younger than the original sample, gave me an opportunity to engage a slightly younger cohort in the research. While most interviewees in the formal study had gained employment prior to the recession, my students are graduating into a workplace that shows signs of a global recession, and this will affect their views. Although I did not conduct formal interviews with the students, I learned a lot from them during in-class discussions and individual consultations. I draw on much of this material alongside the presentations outside of academia that I was allowed to participate in. I was for instance interviewing for a different research project members of one organization who had just undergone diversity training. In the diversity training a colleague and friend of mine had used my research to illustrate some of the generational dynamics. Much of my research was reflected back to me in the research interviews. This allowed the seeing of a true moment of double hermeneutics where we can actually see research-in-action.

Most organizations are keenly interested in what their competitors are doing that might inspire their own practices. This is often called best practice. While best practice is often useful for practitioners to spark ideas about what to do, academic research on best practice is rather sceptical about it. In one piece of research best practice is described rather as a best guess (Kalev, Dobbin & Kelly, 2006). Despite the fact that best practice might not stand up to academic scrutiny, the double hermeneutics approach followed in this book means that those practices are seen as meaningful and worthwhile of academic interpretation. However rather than talking about best practice, I prefer the term signature practice to denote that the practices that individual organizations adopt successfully cannot be transferred to other organizations without a serious consideration of the organizational culture.

In order to share *signature practices* through this book, I will include various vignettes of organizations that have adopted interesting strategies in relation to developing Millennial men and women. Those approaches helped me to think through the practical implications of the theoretical views developed in this book and might be a suitable template for emulation by others. However it should be remembered that organizational change approaches work best when the organizational culture supports a certain initiative. Therefore transplanting one initiative to the next might not lead to the desired results. I nevertheless hope that it could inspire practitioners to think creatively about what they could to bring about change in regard to how they develop the Millennial generation as senior leaders while taking gender into consideration.

This book draws on academic research to explore how Millennial women can be developed as leaders but it is written for a mainly non-academic audience with an interest in the subject. This necessitated a different writing style from a normal academic publication. This means that I will not include as many references as common academic practice and I have chosen to present the empirical material in a more narrative way. I will also explore organizational practices that are signature practices for organizations to highlight how some of the insight generated might have an impact in practice.

STRUCTURE OF THIS BOOK

The structure of the book consists of a more theoretical part where the academic research is reviewed and a more empirical part where I draw on the material collected as part of the research project. The first theoretical part develops the heuristic to think through developing Millennial women as leaders. In the second chapter, I will take a look at gender in the workplace and explore implications for leadership development. In the third chapter, I will review the academic literature on Millennials and again highlight the effects on leadership development. In the fourth chapter I will then take the two different lenses together and review the literature on developing Millennial women as leaders. Although this sounds theoretical, it will provide us with the basis for a substantiated argument on Millennial women.

The subsequent chapters will then explore the different elements of the heuristic in detail by drawing on the empirical research we conducted. Chapter 5 will explore role models for Millennial women. Chapter 6 will analyse why authenticity is important for Millennials and how it can be developed. Chapter 7 will then discuss feedback as a tool for Millennial leadership development. Chapter 8 will explore how formal training can help status transitions through a rite of passage and what happens to gender in this rite of passage. Chapter 9 will explore visibility by discussing networks. Chapter 10 will then highlight the importance of an organizational culture that values work–life integration and where leaders and managers show an awareness for stereotypes. This introduction is then mirrored in a final chapter that brings the insights together and summarizes the findings.

CONCLUSION

In this opening chapter, I have outlined the field of gender, generation and leadership development that is the basis for this book.
The chapter provided some basic definitions of these elements and
started to outline a heuristic that will allow us to think through
gender, Millennials and Millennial women, and leadership development. I explained some basic fundamentals of the methodology as
well as how I have chosen to present the material with the aim of
communicating academic research to a general audience. The structure of the book was explained to guide the reader through the
different chapters.

2

WOMEN AS LEADERS

INTRODUCTION

A female junior professional of South Asian descent in one of the big professional service firms has on the surface the potential to be a senior leader of the future. She is ambitious, she is smart and she enjoys her work. Yet she talked to me about how for her work is a constant process of deciphering. A good example of this is performance evaluation. In order to perform well, she has to 'appropriately challenge' colleagues. However, she is not sure what 'appropriately' means. If she is disagreeing, is her disagreement too strong or not strong enough? As a South Asian woman she was not brought up to dissent with others, particularly not those in superior positions. She is unsure about the desired behavioural patterns that others take for granted and on which her performance is evaluated. The female junior professional from South Asian descent does not know how to correctly challenge a colleague because she lacks the right symbolic capital. For a white, upper-middle class man it might be perfectly clear what this means and how to perform it yet for those who not no fulfil this norm, it might be more tricky. This process of deciphering the organizational culture is something that many women experience on daily basis.

In this chapter, I outline the key challenges for developing women as leaders. I will do this by describing gender segregation in the workplace. I will then outline the rationale for organizations to engage with issues of gender diversity and explore paradigms for gender change. The chapter will culminate in a discussion of the central components of leadership development for women, which will be the first layer of the heuristic to be developed.

GENDER SEGREGATION AT WORK

We live in a time when we often presume that gender no longer matters. Most people can select the jobs they want without legal restrictions on whether women or men are suitable for the job. Slightly more women than men have a university education in Organisation for Economic Co-operation and Development (OECD) countries.[1] Moreover, differences in the employment rate of men and women are falling in nearly all these countries, meaning that many women are increasingly well-educated and in paid employment (OECD, 2012). This supports the belief that gender inequality is a thing of the past, and if it happens, it must happen elsewhere. In sharp contrast to this stands the reality that gender equality is far from being achieved in either the developed or the developing world. The Global Gender Gap Report published by the World Economic Forum in fact shows that no country in the world has achieved gender equality (Hausmann, Tyson & Zahidi, 2011).

At the core of many debates on women in business is so-called gender segregation (Charles, 2003). While women constitute around 50% of entry-level positions, most organizations report that only 30% of their mid-management and 10% of their top management are women (Gratton, Kelan & Walker, 2007). This is called vertical segregation. In addition, horizontal segregation is also widespread, with men and women working in different areas, such as women in nursing and men in software programming. This segregation manifests in various issues that are discussed in relation to women in business. I have classified those issues into five overlapping areas: the gender pay gap; work–life balance; recruitment, selection and promotion; career development and the masculine cultures of organizations.

The *gender pay gap* is widely documented. In the European Union the unadjusted overall pay gap is currently 17.1% (Eurostat, 2011). There is also evidence that the pay gap is stronger at the bottom and the top of the pay scale (Kee, 2006). One commonly suggested explanation for the gender pay gap lies in the fact that women and men tend to work in different areas. For example, while men are more likely to pick high-paying jobs in finance, women tend to choose jobs, such as those in human resources, that pay less well (horizontal segregation). In addition, women seem to occupy less senior positions in organizations (vertical segregation). The pay gap is also partly due to women's different life cycles. However, variables such as the different life cycles of men and women and different occupational choices do not fully explain the pay gap and many agree that gender discrimination also plays an important contributory role (Smith, Smith & Verne, 2010).

It is often argued that women have different life cycles as a result of their familial responsibilities, which means that they often take on flexible working options such as part-time work and focus more on *work–life balance*. Current constructions of the 'ideal worker' are premised on the idea of a full-time worker who is available for the organization at all times and who has no private life (Acker, 1990). Those who work part-time or have commitments outside of work often consequently find themselves side-tracked in organizations. Due to women's care-giving roles, this type of career path is most often allotted to women and is consequently referred to as the 'mummy-track' (Kelan, 2008a). In many cases women are not given the same chances to develop their career when working flexibly.

Recruitment, selection and promotion is another area commonly studied in relation to men and women in business. Much of the research has focused on so-called vertical segregation or the scarcity of women in leadership positions in business. The 50:30:10 rule characterizes the numerical representation of women in organizations: at entry level 50% of the positions are held by women; this decreased to 30% in middle management and to 10% in senior management (Gratton, Kelan & Walker, 2007). The 50:30:10 rule is an example of what is called the 'leaky pipeline'. Different industries are also dominated by one gender, computing, for example, by men and nursing by women. This affects who is attracted to the respective areas.

Research indicates that the *career development* paths of men and women differ. This can relate to the critical abilities that potential leaders have to engage in order to advance, which might include networking, mentoring or training. As this area overlaps to a large degree with leadership development, I will review the literature in this area when developing the heuristic for the book towards the end of this chapter.

The *masculine culture of organizations* also plays a crucial role. The concept of the 'ideal worker' is not only permeating views on flexible working but is also influencing which behaviour is deemed acceptable in organizations (Acker, 1990). In order to fit into the masculine culture of organizations, women often have to manage like a man (Wajcman, 1998). Research in this area has highlighted that both subtle and not-so subtle stereotypes exist about leaders and women's inability to conform to them. This puts women in a double bind. If they manage like a man, they risk not being seen as a woman, but if they are seen as a woman, they risk not being seen as a manager. This masculine ideal makes it difficult for women to advance in organizations.

The area of gender in organizations is complex and this deliberately brief review should indicate how intertwined the issues of gender in the workplace are. This also shows that in such a complex network finding a single solution to resolve those gender issues is going to be difficult. In this book, we will therefore develop a much more focused approach by specifically exploring leadership development of junior women in organizations.

THE BUSINESS CASE FOR GENDER DIVERSITY

While we have established that gender discrimination continues to exist, the question is why organizations should care about this. Traditionally, three different cases were put forward to explain organizational engagement with gender equality. First, the *legal case* for gender equality ensures through laws and regulations that women and men are not disadvantaged in any way. The law is of course based on social conventions translated into law; that gender equality is enshrined in law indicates that society as a whole feels it is important. However we shall not forget that gender equality legislation varies greatly around the world. Having the right and enforcing it are also different issues. For instance, many women who feel discriminated at work would shy away from a lawsuit because they know that this often means the end of their professional career because other companies might be unwilling to hire a 'troublemaker'. In addition, gender discrimination has in times of political correctness moved underground and is often more subtle and more difficult to detect. This however does not mean that traditional forms of gender discrimination have completely gone away.

Second, the *social case* proclaims that the lack of women in leadership positions is essentially a question of social justice. If women are not able to make a contribution to decision making at higher levels, then society as a whole is seen as not functioning well. The egalitarian values that are upheld elsewhere in society are not brought to bear, which means that society does not fulfil its self-created standards. The argument would also suggest that societal functioning can be enhanced by having women in greater number in decision-making positions.

For most organizations the *business case* is the main driver for paying attention to gender in the workplace. The term *business case* could be replaced with excellence or efficiency case in a non-commercial setting. The business case essentially refers to the relationship between organizational performance and gender diversity. The underlying assumption is that businesses exist to make profit and unless gender diversity is linked to profit decision makers within organizations are not going to support initiatives on gender diversity.

There are various points to consider in researching the business case for gender diversity. First, it is important to distinguish between tangible and intangible business benefits. Tangible business benefits refer mainly to financial performance. Yet other issues that might be crucial for organizations relate to innovation and creativity. Since they are intangible, they are harder to measure. Second, it is important to distinguish between studies that show a business case for gender diversity and those that explore diversity overall. The effects one might see for gender, will not necessarily be true for ethnicity or disability. Third, often a causal link between two events is assumed but not proven. One might for instance find that financial performance increases when more women are on the board, but it has to be carefully assessed as to how far one is related to the other. It could for instance be that companies that do better financially decide to take a 'risk' by getting more women on their board, which counteracts the common interpretation that women on the board lead to better performance. Finally, there is often also a question about the veracity of the evidence. If studies are motivated to show that gender diversity is good for business, they might be inclined to disregard evidence that suggests the opposite. This does not mean that the studies showing the business case for gender diversity are not valid, but it cautions us to take a careful look at how the studies were conducted.

From a more academic perspective, there is little evidence that there is a solid business case for diversity as a whole. A long-term project at the Massachusetts Institute of Technology has found limited evidence for the fact that business performance and overall diversity are linked (Kochan et al., 2003). Other academic research has shown that diversity does not necessarily increase performance or the talent pool (Jayne & Dipboye, 2004).

While this research looked at overall diversity, there is also interesting research on the business case for women. A good example is an academic study on how orchestras adapted to the inclusion of women over time (Allmendinger & Hackman, 1995). The research looked at four orchestras in four different countries to explore the effects an increasing proportion of women has on orchestras. The researchers measured perspectives on the functioning of orchestras, the quality of members' relationships and their satisfaction and motivation. While most people are led to believe that gender diversity has positive effects, the study showed the contrast. In fact, it is shown that as the number of women increases, the four areas studied deteriorated. However this negative trend stopped when gender parity was achieved, that is, when men and women approached 50%

each in the orchestras. Then the trend flattened or was positive. This shows that gender diversity might not immediately improve performance but its effects might only unfold in the long-term.

Our research focused on innovation and we were interested in how teams scored in regard to certain innovation behaviour within different proportions of men and women (Gratton et al., 2007). Our data set contained teams with only women, only men and various proportions in between. Our innovation indicators included self-confidence, experimentation, efficiency and psychological safety (the latter refers to an environment for interpersonal risk taking). We found that those teams who had 50% men and 50% women scored best in regard to their innovation behaviour.

The business case and the social case for gender diversity have for a long time been seen as competing rationales for engaging in gender diversity. However, the most recent thinking on corporate social responsibility has offered an alternative to this perspective. It is now increasingly argued that improving gender diversity is not only beneficial for society but also equally beneficial for the bottom line. The idea of 'shared value' indicates the transformative potential emanating from reconceptualizing the relationship between improving society and ameliorating business performance (Porter & Kramer, 2011). A similar type of thinking increasingly also starts to permeate thinking on gender diversity, which means that the social case and the business case are increasingly converging. Therefore, improving gender diversity is seen as enhancing business performance and social performance.

Although the research evidence to support the hypothesis that diversity enhances performance is at best inconclusive, it appears that most organizations today accept that diversity, and particularly gender diversity, is vital for their sustainability. And they are eager to change the current situation. Academic research has devised some guidance on how initiatives that attempt to change gender and diversity in organizations can be brought to fruition (Jayne & Dipboye, 2004). This includes being aware that the benefits of the change campaign will be contingent on the situation. In order to be successful the diversity initiatives need to be project-managed with specific deliverables staggered to be completed in the short-, medium- and long-term. The framing of the initiative is important, which means talking about challenges and opportunities rather than threats. It is also important to secure leadership commitment and accountability for the change initiative. The change approach needs to be tailored to the issue that is to be solved, which normally means conducting a needs assessment.

For most organizations the business case for gender equality is seen as the main driver to engagement in change processes in regard to gender diversity. While there is limited academic evidence for an overall business case for diversity, it is important to highlight that benefits to business from gender and diversity are most likely to occur if they are specific, project managed carefully and framed in such a way to allow change to happen.

FRAMING GENDER

Given the fact that framing is so important for processes of gender and diversity change, it is useful to look at how gender change campaigns are normally framed. In my research and work with organizations I found three different ways of framing gender change campaigns: making women more like men, building on gender difference and widening the template.

First, organizations try to *make women more like men*. Making women more like men means that women are made fit into career structures that were designed with men in mind. This would mean excluding any parameters that can make women potentially different. It usually encompasses a lot of focus on managing maternity and how to get enough support to ensure that normal working life is not impeded by the private life. A classic example would the high-flying senior professional woman who sees her kids for 30 minutes in the morning and the rest of the day the children are cared for by various nannies and helpers, allowing her to work as long as she needs to and to go on any last-minute business trips without concern. Here any difference between men and women is ignored or made to disappear through a fine-tuned set of arrangements. In this approach gender is made not to matter by women complying with a male-model career plan.

Second, organizations start to recognize and *value gender difference*. In this approach it is assumed that men and women are different, either based on biology and/or socialization, and hence bring different things to their work. Organizations would start developing flexible career paths for women to allow them to combine the different responsibilities they have in their lives. In addition, these organizations would see a great benefit from differences. An example of such an approach is the widely repeated idea that the testosterone of Wall Street and the City of London led to the global financial meltdown. High testosterone in the morning has been linked to higher returns over the day for male traders (Coates & Herbert, 2008). However if testosterone is regularly high, this increases the risks that male traders take (Coates, Gurnell & Sarnyai, 2010). Given that men have higher levels of testosterone than women, the argument is that women would be more risk adverse and hence would not have gambled with funds to the same degree. An organization in this stage would argue that women would make more prudent decisions and should therefore be hired and promoted. This however ignores the strong socialization factors that are present in these organizations: people are hired and promoted based on the risks they take because this is where profit lies. Recruiting women into a system that encourages risky behaviour means that only those women who are comfortable taking risks survive and the others leave. If we believe the research on which this argument is based, the numbers that stay will not be many.

This is why the third approach focuses more on systems. It is often presumed that the template of the ideal worker in an organization needs to be changed, but I prefer to talk about *widening the template* to allow more individuals to appear as ideal workers. This approach does not look at women. It explores the academic concept of the 'ideal worker'. This concept highlights that an organization hires and promotes a certain type of person (Acker, 1990). This would mean observing what an organization looks for in an ideal worker, and which traits, skills and behaviours the ideal worker shows. In most organizations there are clear ideas of what promotable candidates look like. Most organizations would argue that they are gender neutral and every candidate can succeed. In reality many of our practices are governed, often subconsciously, by stereotypical perceptions. While we are aware of surface stereotypes, most of our stereotypes actually reside in the subconscious. However in order to react to those stereotypes it is important that we move them from the subconscious to the conscious level, that is, we have to become aware of them. Research has shown that stereotypes can be made conscious by addressing them directly (that means to speak about them) and by seeing people counteracting the stereotype (Roberson et al., 2003). The key challenge is to become aware of the ideal worker stereotype in the first instance, which will then help to widen it.

A good example of the effects of the ideal worker is discussed at the beginning of the chapter. If the female junior professional of South Asian descent is not sure what 'appropriately challenging' means behaviourally, it is difficult for her to put it into practice. She lacks the right symbolic capital and will therefore never be the ideal worker. Rather than explaining to women how to engage in certain behaviour or accepting that women are just different, this approach tackles the root cause by asking for whom is the template designed.

The key is then to widen the template to allow different people to become the ideal worker rather than relying on a restrictive view of who can be an ideal worker.

The fundamental issue for gender in organizations is that organizations were designed by men and with men in mind. Moreover the generic man is also white, able-bodied, middle-aged and usually upper-middle class as well. The model of organizations that we have long followed is one that fits an industrial economy. However, this traditional model of an organization does not appear to be particularly suited for the challenges and opportunities of doing business in the networked knowledge economy. The ideal worker that defined the standard for organizations in the past will no longer serve organizations well as they move into the future. It is evident that those organizations who widen the template of people they employ will be sustainable in the future. This means that the lack of women in senior positions in organizations is only the symptom of a much deeper root cause that has to be tackled.

A GENDERED APPROACH TO LEADERSHIP DEVELOPMENT

Many people argue that the under-representation of women in senior positions is just a matter of time; it will even out over time as women gain university degrees and become more present in the workforce (OECD, 2012). It is argued that high achieving women will push through any residues of the glass ceiling that still might hinder their progression. However, this view is a bit naïve in that just doing nothing might not lead to the required results. If organizations are designed to allow only people who fit certain templates through, they will just clone their existing population of employees and senior leaders. For too long organizations have relied on such cloning, but this will not be enough to compete in the future. In order to substantiate this point, it is useful to take a closer look at some of the associated challenges in regard to current leadership development practices. Let's go back to the heuristic I introduced in the previous chapter. This will allow us to focus on six elements that I have identified as being critical for leadership development, in order to explore them from a gendered perspective. These are: role models, authenticity, experiential learning, formal education, visibility and organizational culture. I derived the six elements from the literature on leadership development (Day, 2000; Groves, 2007; Hopkins et al., 2008). As I explained in the last chapter, the six can be summarized into three categories (self-knowledge, acquiring knowledge and social knowledge) to form the basis of the heuristic.

Let's start by looking at the category of self-knowledge. One of the most common reasons cited for the lack of female leaders is that there are just not enough mentors, sponsors and role models for women. It is useful to first of all differentiate between mentors and role models. Mentoring is usually seen as requiring consent from the mentor to engage in an interactive relationship. A mentor helps in navigating organizational politics and increases the mentee's sense of self-confidence through developmental feedback (Ragins & Cotton, 1999). While mentoring relationships can evolve on any hierarchical level, sponsorship relationships imply a more senior sponsor who promotes the protégée and thereby advances him or her (Ibarra, Carter & Silva, 2010). In order to be a role model a person just has to identify with another person; the other person might not even know this.

Role models, sponsors and mentors can all provide ways of identification. Identification is a process through which individuals shape their own identity by taking in something of the person they identify with. In order for this identification to be successful sameness based on a chosen category, such as being a woman, is usually seen as beneficial. However, with few senior women around, it is argued that women lack the opportunity to identify with more senior women in the workplace. This would mean that in order to for women to develop as leaders they need to be able to identify with senior women as role models, mentors and sponsors.

Second, authenticity. Authenticity is often described as self-awareness (Sparrowe, 2005) but can also be seen as an awareness of others (Maak & Pless, 2006). Being aware of the self and others is seen as important to one's perception as a leader. This commonly involves blending the professional and private spheres and is often equated with 'being yourself' at work. While authenticity is often a desired characteristic in organizations, it appears that this authenticity is not the way leadership talent is identified. Future leaders are often selected based on the template of those who are currently in those positions. If leadership development is designed to replace the ideal leader, who is more likely than not to be a man, then it might be difficult to develop future female leaders. Women are then just seen as not fitting the template and will be perceived as lacking the right skills to succeed. Moreover, as we have seen in the previous section, stereotypes also play a major role here. Even if women might have skills suitable for the role, they are perceived as not right for the job because they do not perform those skills in the right way. In addition, in a frustrating double bind, women are often perceived as not authentic if they perform a leadership role, which is seen as masculine.

In order to avoid women slipping under the radar when it comes to identifying future leaders, it is therefore important to devise systems and practices that ensure that women are included. When it comes to training and promotion, it is for instance important to practise affirmative search. Affirmative search means that an organization seeks a diverse slate of candidates without necessarily trying to fill a quota. This is well-known for external hires and it can also be practised internally where for every position a balanced shortlist may be required. For leadership development that means that the number of women is monitored. In many organizations leadership development only starts in earnest in middle management positions when people are in their 30s. However, from the perspective of a woman's life cycle, many women will by that time have 'de-selected' themselves from that high potential pool or have become 'invisible' due to what are (from a the perspective of a male life cycle) non-normative work patterns, including freelance and flexible working.

In regard to acquiring knowledge, experiential learning or on the job learning is a commonly used tool for leadership development. This can involve internal courses, action learning, international assignments or stretch assignments that allow aspiring leaders to gain experience and feedback from different situations. These critical experiential learning activities are often not monitored from a gender perspective (Gratton, Kelan & Walker, 2007). If an organization wants to develop women leaders, it is vitally important to ensure not only that high potentials are undergoing developmental activities but also that women get the right exposure to developing these central skills. It is often assumed that women do not want to participate in those experiences and so they are therefore not offered. Rather than presuming that women do not want those experiences, it is important to avoid those assumptions and have open conversations with women on this topic. Once women have entered experiential learning experiences it is also important that they receive critical feedback to improve their performance.

Formal education in the form of an MBA or executive development has long been seen as a way to develop leadership potential. Such formal education aims at helping the transition from being a junior person in an organization to being a more senior person. These training courses do not only allow individuals to acquire technical skills about management. They also allow the participants self-reflexivity, which means that they can critically think about themselves and others. In most MBA classrooms women only constitute just over 30% of the class in top MBA programmes (*Financial*

Times, 2012), and this number has not changed significantly in the last decade in spite of various initiatives to increase the number of women on those courses (Kelan & Dunkley Jones, 2010). The picture is even more bleak in tailor-made executive programmes, where many organizations send only very few women. This means that women are in minority positions and the special concerns of women as a group are not considered. Some authors argue that women-only programmes are a useful way of developing women leaders through reflecting on their leadership style in general and in relation to their gender (Vinnicombe & Singh, 2003). There are various successful women-only programmes run for instance by Simmons College in the US (see Chapter 8) and by INSEAD in France. While these programmes certainly develop women as leaders, I have argued that it is also important to make mainstream management education more gender aware (Kelan & Dunkley Jones, 2010). This would ensure that all future leaders, men as well as women, grasp the importance of diversity. This would allow them to better manage in a gender-aware way. This means that apart from monitoring the number of women attending in-class teaching, it is also important to modify the content of the teaching sessions to be gender aware.

The final category relates to social knowledge. Potential leaders need to be visible in order to succeed, as it is the lack of visibility that leads to talented individuals being overlooked when it comes to leadership development. This visibility means ensuring that the potential leader appears on the radar of more people than the individual line manager. This visibility is often achieved through networks. It is presumed that people like to associate us with others who are more like us, a human trait which is called homophily. Homophily can express itself in relation to gender, class and race as well as other dimensions based on which similarity can be perceived. Many organizations presume that what women lack are networks to reach the top. This is due to the fact that homophily works against women. As most senior leaders are men, those men are likely to recruit in their own image and to give jobs to people who are more like themselves. This is widely referred to as the 'old boys' network'. To counteract the old boys' network women's networks within organizations and outside of organizations are seen by many organizations as a quick fix for providing women with networks allowing them to climb the organizational hierarchy.

The last, but not least element is the organizational culture. Organizational cultures are governed by many unspoken 'rules', which are shared assumptions about how work is done. This organizational culture expresses itself for instance in how the boundary between work and life is constructed, which is often said to be particularly important for potential women leaders. The organizational culture will also eulogize an ideal worker and be imbued by stereotypes. In general, the culture of the organization needs to support leadership development. This often means that the CEO, senior leadership and mid-level managers must visibly support leadership development. Developing others should be a key component of job descriptions and performance evaluation for top and mid-level management. This might for instance include rewarding existing managers and leaders for developing women.

CONCLUSION

This chapter fulfilled a dual purpose. First it outlined some central insights into gender in organizations by exploring critical areas, the business case for gender diversity and the framing of gender change. These insights were then used to look more closely at a heuristic for developing women as leaders. This heuristic consists of six elements: role models, authenticity, experiential learning, formal learning, visibility and organizational culture, which were discussed from a gendered perspective. This constitutes the first layer of the heuristic for developing Millennial leaders. In the next chapter, the research on Millennials is discussed with a view to developing the next layer of this heuristic.

3

MILLENNIALS AS LEADERS

INTRODUCTION

Justin is a business student who graduated in 2012. This appears to be a tough year in which to graduate due to the tight labour market. However, Justin is an excellent student and during his final year had three job offers with prestigious companies to choose from: a major professional services firm, a large technology management consultancy and a small management consultancy. For Justin deciding between the three offers was not easy. What influenced his decision was his future development. He could not see much point in joining the professional services firm or the large management consultancy because it would take eight to ten years to make partner. This was just too long for him. He liked the small management consultancy because they offered him a fast-track career, but he was concerned that this would mean not to have a big brand on his CV. In the end, Justin decided to join the professional service firm because that would give him a big brand on his CV and enhance his skills but he did not expect to stick around for longer than one or two years before moving on to pastures new.

While for previous generations the three job offers would have appeared a brilliant start to a career, and waiting eight to ten years to become partner was not a long time, this has changed for the Millennial generation. Even if organizations attract new talent, they feel that they leave too quickly, not allowing enough time for them to be developed as leaders. This means high attrition costs and a fundamental challenge to the pyramid-style format of many organizations. Is it really true that this generation thinks and acts differently, and if so, why is this the case? This chapter will trace some of the changes that differentiate Millennials from other generations. We will also explore some apparent contradictions that are emerging in the profile of Millennials by drawing on wider societal changes that influence them. We will explore if this generation makes different

31

choices to previous ones not by stereotyping them but instead by understanding the *Zeitgeist* that formed this generation's mindset. I will then progress to add an additional layer to the heuristic, which will consider how Millennials can be developed as leaders.

RESEARCHING CHANGING GENERATIONS

The latest generation to enter the workplace has many names: Generation Y, Millennials, Net Gen, Generation Next, to name but few. In addition to this plethora of names, there is an equally confusing array of birth years this generation seems to span. No surprise then that many people find the field of generations at work confusing. There are three ways to describe a generation: the age-based definition, the cohort-based definition and the incumbency-based definition (Joshi et al., 2010). I have argued that all three definitions will be used in this book. In terms of the age group, I am focusing on individuals who were born between 1977 and 1987, which corresponds to the early tranche of the Millennial generation. Some of the informal interviews were also with individuals who were born in the early 1990s. In terms of cohort-based identities, the main focus of the book are people who either entered business school or organizations at around the same time. Finally, in regard to incumbency-based definitions, the subjects that feature in this book are mostly in the junior ranks of organizations or are undergoing the transition from a junior person to a more senior person. With this definition in mind, it is useful to take a closer look at some of the academic research on generations.

While there is a lot of literature on generational differences, much of this literature seems to originate from practitioner research. This research is insightful but sometimes entails problems, particularly in relation to methodology. Methodologically it is difficult to establish generational differences while avoiding measuring life stage. If one would for instance ask Millennials, Generation X and Baby Boomers about their attitudes, behaviours and preferences, they would answer from their current life stage perspective. Baby Boomers approaching retirement and Generation X professionals trying to climb the corporate ladder while building their families will probably have a different perspective on life than Millennials who are just making their first experiences in the workplace. In order to achieve an unbiased view one needs to ask the same questions of Millennials, Generation X and Baby Boomers when they were aged 20 to 25. Only by doing that, is it possible to discern real changes in attitudes that are generational (and not based on age).

The problem is obviously that few studies can span 30 to 40 years, and even then it would only be a single study. A great alternative are cross-temporal meta-analyses. Meta-analysis is a statistical method that in simple terms combines the results of different studies and look at common findings. This avoids looking only at the findings of one study. For generational research cross-temporal meta-analyses are very useful because they look at the results of different studies across time. Often similar scales are used, which essentially means that the same questions are asked in different studies across time. These time-lag studies can show differences between generations and not just ages. Most of those studies seem to be based on tracking university students – a convenient data set for many university professors – following graduation and through their careers. Most of the studies are also conducted in the United States of America, which means that the global situation might differ from this. Nevertheless cross-temporal meta-analyses are one of the best ways academically to detect generational differences.

Research based on cross-temporal meta-analyses is best suited to highlighting generational differences. It is important to keep in mind that those studies describe averages and there will always be individual differences (Twenge & Campbell, 2008). Rather than stereotyping these studies measure how an average young person from today differs from an average young person from another generation. These studies are designed to detect differences, which means that even though there are many similarities across generations the focus will be on what is actually different (Twenge & Campbell, 2008).

GENERATIONAL TRAIT CHANGES

What cross-temporal meta-analyses show is that trait changes are not sudden but happen over time (Twenge & Campbell, 2008). In the studies discussed further in the chapter, the birth years of Millennials or Generation Me ranges from the mid-1970s to 1982. Let's start by looking at five areas where trait changes between one generation and another have been observed: self-esteem and narcissism, need for social approval, locus of control, anxiety and depression, and changes in women's roles and personalities.

Research has indicated a range of trait changes that can be observed in Millennials. Let's start by looking at *self-esteem and narcissism*, which has gone up (Twenge & Campbell, 2008). Overall, it should be a positive sign that people perceive their own worth as higher but self-love or being self-centred are often seen as less posi-tive traits. The downside is that Millennials can be overconfident.

This becomes evident in relation to narcissism. Narcissism can often sound derogatory in every day use but it is used in psychological research to capture certain attributes. Here narcissism means that one has high self-esteem and feels entitled. Narcissism also often means that one wants to be famous and wealthy. With the rise of social media and reality TV many Millennials seem to believe that they, too, can become famous and grow up in a society that finds this kind of fame laudable. Research shows that people high in narcissism are more likely to take risks and their performance has more peaks and valleys. Employees who have a high self-esteem might also be more defensive when receiving criticism. This trait change might explain why Millennials expect more from their workplace than their parents, particularly in terms of the meaning of their work. Millennials also appreciate authenticity, and if a workplace does not meet their expectations in regard to allowing them to be themselves at work, they are less likely to compromise and more likely to leave the organization.

Organizations mainly respond to these generational changes by setting individual expectations and meeting regularly for feedback. Feedback is crucial for this generation and should be celebrated more to feed self-esteem. An inflated concept of the self, might also lead to the impression that Millennials can do everything they want and having many options makes it also more difficult to make a decision. I will discuss this risk of making the wrong choices later. For organizations this means that self-evaluations will become less helpful to assess employees but 360-degree feedback can fill this void. With their appreciation of authenticity Millennials will also appreciate authentic leaders. Leaders are increasingly questioned over their behaviour; only if they convince Millennials of their integrity they will be accepted as leaders.

The second trait change relates to the need for *social approval*, which has declined (Twenge & Campbell, 2008). Social approval means how concerned an individual is to make a good impression on others and how likely they are to conform. Millennials are less concerned about the impression they make on others, which is indicated in their informal dress. While informal dress works well for companies like Google, more conservative companies like banks will struggle with Millennials not conforming to their dress code. Declining social approval also means also that Millennials do not like conformity and prefer to do things in new ways. It is exactly these new ideas and fresh perspectives that many Millennials are not shy to voice that many organizations value highly for innovation and creativity. As social approval becomes less important changing jobs frequently is also no longer perceived as a stigma – if one does not care much about other people's opinion about oneself then surely one does not mind that others look down on one's decision to change jobs frequently. Instead Millennials seem to be the first generation to fully appreciate new forms of careers that are based on a portfolio of projects (discussed further later). However, research has also shown that as job security seems to be becoming a thing of the past, Millennials ironically value job security more than previous generations (Twenge, 2010). This might be the case because they know that job security is hard to get. As we will see later on, this means that Millennials will not leave their jobs when they have the feeling that they can grow and develop in their organization.

The third trait change is that the *locus of control* is more *external* (Twenge & Campbell, 2008). What does this mean? An external locus of control describes the mentality that one has little impact on how events unfold. An internal locus of control, however, means that one feels in control of shaping events. Millennials do – on average – believe that they have little impact on events themselves, that decisions are made by others and that much depends on luck. This means that when things go wrong they tend to blame others, attribute the outcome to luck and are unlikely to take responsibility for failures. Organizations should therefore stress the support they are giving Millennials, which will strengthen their organizational commitment and satisfaction. Interestingly, this might also explain why Millennials are seen as preferring collaborative work styles; if more individuals contribute and the locus of control is external, then the chances of success are seen as higher. Working in teams means that one shares accountability and rewards and losses. However this needs to be balanced with individual work so as also to feed the need of Millennials for recognition and affirmation. While cross-temporal meta-analyses stress that the focus of control is more external, the concept of individualization that we will discuss later in this chapter actually presumes that individuals feel greater responsible to create themselves in times when life courses are themselves changing.

Anxiety and depression are more common in the Millennial generation than in previous generations (Twenge & Campbell, 2008). Research has indicated that anxiety and depression are higher in young adolescents and children today, and this trend continues when people enter the workplace. Modern workplaces are often experienced as stressful. Work has to be completed in ever shorter periods of time, work hours are getting longer, people are expected to be more productive and jobs are increasingly insecure. It is also important to remember that while some stress is useful and positive to maintain top performance, too much stress is dangerous and will lead to 'burn out', with negative effects on work performance. For Millennials ambiguity presents a major element of stress. Millennials dislike ambiguity and regularly want clarification from their employers (and their professors as far as exams and coursework are concerned!). For organizations this means strengthening their work–life balance programmes and creating more clarity about the roles that junior professionals are expected to play in the organization. Again, feedback-giving mechanisms are particularly important for this generation because they might help mitigate some of the stress associated with ambiguity. It is interesting to note that while cross-temporal meta-analyses have shown that Millennials have more self-esteem, they are also more anxious and depressed. I will offer an explanation for this phenomenon later on when I draw on individualization to explore these tensions and incongruencies further.

Finally, and centrally important for this book, are changes in *women's roles and personalities* (Twenge & Campbell, 2008). Women have entered the labour market en masse in recent decades and research has observed a rise in women's assertiveness. Moreover it can be observed that women now show many of the traits that for a long period of time were associated with masculinity, such as assertiveness. Today female university students on average score as well as men in assertiveness. Interestingly, we do not see the same changes in scorings of feminine-connoted skills like nurturing and compassion, which are still mainly associated with women. This is due to the fact that while women have entered the labour market and have adopted traditionally masculine-connoted skills, the same cannot be said for men. While women's roles have changed drastically in recent decades, men's roles did not change as much. Men have not moved into domestic care work in significant numbers, which might explain why men have not adopted more feminine connoted traits.[1]

While women in the West now do as well if not better than men in education and are increasingly taking leadership roles within business, gender ideals and stereotypes still hold sway. Research has not found any significant differences in the leadership style of men and women (Eagly & Karau, 1991), yet often women are expected to be better listeners and better collaborators. Women leaders are expected to excel in social skills. Those stereotypes continue to limit women in leadership positions. They also hinder men because they presume that men cannot develop a collaborative leadership style. It is also true that many women still work the double burden of paid labour and domestic labour, which puts additional pressure on their work–life balance. This means that first of all, organizations need to continue to foster stereotype awareness training and they do need to address work–life balance issues to allow women to unfold their leadership potential and allow men to bring a more balanced perspective to their work.

All in all, Millennials have higher self-esteem, which might mean that they are overconfident and might struggle to accept criticism. They are less likely to conform and value authenticity, which might explain why Millennials move on if they can no longer be themselves in an organization. Millennials on average are more likely to think that they have little impact on success or failure and are therefore less likely to take responsibility for failures and are keen to share this risk with others through teamwork. Millennials have higher anxiety levels. While this might give them the edge to perform better, it might also lead to burn out. Ambiguity makes them feel more stressed and feedback can help to mitigate this stress. Millennial women are as assertive as their male counterparts but Millennial men have not taken on more feminine connoted traits. Stereotypes and work–life balance issues are a particular factor that might hinder women's leadership development. This short profile of this generation provides an excellent backdrop for further exploration into what makes Millennials tick. Before exploring why these trait changes might have come about, it is useful to focus a bit more on how Millennials can be incentivized.

WORK–LIFE BALANCE AND SOCIAL RESPONSIBILITY

While work–life balance is often discussed as an issue for working mothers, there is clear evidence that the trait changes of the Millennial generation include changes in attitudes to work–life balance. It has been shown that Millennials place more value on leisure than previous generations, which is linked to the often cited desire of Millennials for work–life balance (Twenge et al., 2010). However, the same research also shows that Millennials value extrinsic rewards. This means that while they do want to have leisure time, they also want more money and status, which in turn is linked to their sense of entitlement and higher self-esteem (as discussed in the previous section).

Millennials are also said to be driven to give back to society and want meaning in their work. While it is often assumed that

Millennials value giving back, research has not shown an increase in altruistic values (Twenge et al., 2010). While, as with any generations, some individuals are more altruistic than others, appealing to Millennials' altruistic values will not lead to a higher resonance. Millennials rate money, image and fame (extrinsic values) over than self-acceptance, affiliation and community (intrinsic values) (Twenge et al., 2010; Twenge, Campbell & Freeman, 2012). Millennials show less concern for others through, for instance, having a job that is worthwhile for society and for helping the environment. However we will see in Chapter 10 that Millennials enjoy volunteering work not because of their altruistic values or because they want to do something that is worthwhile for society and the environment but because it allows them to create social bonds which are otherwise in short supply.

From this we can conclude that work–life balance initiatives that seek to enhance the leisure value of Millennials are going to be popular with this generation. However work–life initiatives are all too often seen as supporting working mothers (and in some instances working fathers). Those work–life balance initiatives as well as rewards in terms of time off, while be highly valued by Millennials (Twenge et al., 2010). Initiatives that focus on the meaning of work or volunteering in the community or for the environment will not be a main driver for the average Millennial, but higher pay and more leisure time might keep them happy. Receiving sabbaticals for travel, for instance, would feed Millennials' wish for leisure time. This will in turn help to keep them satisfied and therefore less likely to move jobs.

Let's take another look at the profile of our average Millennial: confident, authentic, anxious (particularly in face of ambiguity), assertive, money-driven, loves leisure time and values job security. The average Millennial is also less altruistic than previous generations. Motivation through monetary rewards and leisure time will resonate with this generation. However, the average Millennial also seems to embody many contradictions: they are more anxious and depressed but also have high self-esteem; they appear disloyal to organizations yet seem to value job security. After developing this profile of a Millennial, it is worthwhile digging a bit deeper to explore why Millennials show some of these traits and what might explain these apparent contradictions.

INDIVIDUALIZATION AND THE QUARTER-LIFE CRISIS

Exploring the psychological traits of an average Millennial is useful to distinguishing the myth of how Millennials are 'supposed to be' from what research has found. However, the changes in psychological traits do not tell us much about the root causes for why Millennials show those traits. In addition, many of the traits seem to be conflicting. It is therefore worthwhile moving from psychology, which traditionally looks at individuals, to sociology, which explores individuals within the societal context. Exploring a more sociological angle will facilitate insight into why this generation has developed those traits and what the rationale for some of those traits and their apparent conflict is. This rationale is linked to the changing nature of the labour market.

Many social theorists have written about the changing nature of the world of work, which will enhance our understanding of the root causes of the trait changes observed in Millennials. One of the most influential theories in sociology over the last decades is that of individualization. Individualization refers to a situation where individuals are increasingly required to shape their own lives (Beck, Giddens & Lash, 1994). We live in a time when life courses appear no longer determined by the 'choice' of individuals. In earlier times lives appeared more predetermined: if one was born the son of a shoemaker one was likely to become a shoemaker oneself or to pick a similar trade. One was likely to stay in the same village or town and life close to one's wider family. Women's choices were even more restricted. However, today many paths appear open to us: we do not have to follow the trade of our fathers (or mothers) but we can; we can stay in the same town where we grew up or move to the other side of the world; and even once we have made the choice of what to do for a living or who to marry, those choices appear much more contingent with people having different careers and divorce rates rising. Millennials growing up in a globalized world where communication and travel shrink distances might be forgiven for thinking that the world is their oyster and what they do when they grow up is entirely their own choosing.

However, in reality our choices are restricted by our class, ethnicity, gender, location in the world and so on. Even though in most Western countries women and people of all skin tones can enter the employment of their choosing, the barriers to entry have moved from external barriers to more internal ones. Depending on our background certain options might just not appear on our radar or are judged as inappropriate for us. Let's take for instance the example of women in the areas of science, engineering and technology. While women in theory can study those subjects, very few women do. Women often claim not be interested in those subjects and hence do not study them (Faulkner, 2000). Many young women in fact judge a career in science, engineering and technology as not suitable for them because it does not fit with the identity they wish to construct. These areas of work are seen as masculine and for many women being interested in them or studying them appears as to conflict with their desired identity as a woman (Kelan, 2009b). By judging certain areas of work as more suitable for us, we recreate societal patterns (and gendered patterns), which in turn constrains our choices of who we can be.

Those constraints appear to be due down to choice, but choice itself is conditioned by society. We often think that our choices are our own and we make them without the influence of others. However, many sociologists have shown for years that our choices are actually influenced by society. We do not make choices in a vacuum but we make choices that we think others might approve. We have seen this earlier on in relation to social approval. However it is important to remember that even stating not to care much for social approval and to make choices that are actively disapproved by society is in fact a choice made vis-à-vis society. Society itself regularly changes and what might appear as a move to lead to social disapproval might change over time. If we think for instance about tattoos, they were once reserved to sailors and people who were rebellious (Blanchard, 1991). However for Millennials tattoos have little to do with rebellion and have rather become a fashion statement that even the most conservatives of Millennials would not see it as breaking societal norms. Tattoos have become societally accepted. When we talk about choice we need to be aware of the fact that choice itself happens in relation to societal norms and values.

Moreover, as we perceive a free choice of who we want to be, this also comes with the added risk of making the wrong choices. While sociologists would readily tell you that choice happens in relation to societal norms and values, for many individuals it does not feel that way. They think that are able to make their own choices on what is best for them. With this belief in making choices and shaping one's own destiny, which is the common perspective in individualization, also comes the risk of making the wrong choices. Whereas before we might have claimed that society is responsible for the choices made, today it is in the individual who shoulders the risk of making the right decision (Beck, 1992). If a wrong choice is made, it is the individual who is responsible.

This is in direct conflict with what we have learned from the cross-temporal meta-analyses, where Millennials were seen as more likely to have an external locus of control. This meant that they do not perceive that they have much impact on how their own success and failure because the outcome is decided elsewhere. Individualization, however, means that people feel they shoulder the risk of making the right or wrong decisions. If one feels personally responsible for making the right or wrong choice this will increase anxiety, which is a trait change that has been supported by cross-temporal meta-analyses. While the locus of control might contradict individualization, the increased anxiety seems to support it. One explanation might be that Millennials feel that they are in charge of creating their own life which makes their decisions important. At the same time they feel unable to determine the outcome of their decisions, which are made somewhere else. If one has to make decisions about one's life, yet is unable to control how these decisions turn out, one will feel more anxious. This would be an explanation as to why the apparent contradictions might be part of a wider, more consistent framework of sense-making.

The so-called quarter-life crisis that seems to hit younger people in their 20s and early 30s seems to be an example of how choice and the responsibilities of making the 'right' choices leaves Millennials in a state of self-questioning. The quarter-life crisis is named after the much discussed mid-life crisis (Atwood & Scholtz, 2008). While the mid-life crisis is the time one reflects on one's life in around middle age, a similar phenomenon seems to happen for younger people when they reach their 20s and early 30s and start reflecting on their own life. The plethora of choices to be made and to be responsible for is linked to the rise in anxiety and depression found in cross-temporal meta-analyses.

We have seen that from industrialization through to the development of the knowledge economy, knowledge became one of the prized commodities required to compete successfully. Education is thus more and more important. With many Millennials completing their higher education in their early 20s, many will spend the next decade establishing themselves professionally, having children later on in life. Their relationships will be more contingent (Allmendinger, 2009). This in itself is a consequence of individualization and the perception that societal approval for less traditional lifestyle arrangements matter less. While one might believe that this decade of establishing oneself in the workplace is a time of relative freedom, Millennials, particularly in the UK and the US, are forced to move back with their families because they cannot afford to live on their own and they are burdened with the high costs of financing their education (Atwood & Scholtz, 2008). The decade in which Millennials try to enter the labour market is the one in which they are most prone to be riddled with self-doubt on whether or not the right decisions were made. In other words, that is when the quarter-life crisis strikes.

The quarter-life crisis is essentially a process of finding and modifying one's identity in the world. Many Millennials find that the ideals and norms they had while growing up no longer fit their adult world (Robbins & Wilner, 2001). This is a time when younger people lack guidance on how to live their lives, which is partly due to the fact that the lifestyles of their parents no longer seem to fit their own ambitions and dreams (Atwood & Scholtz, 2008). As children they have seen that in many cases nuclear families can break apart. Many of the Millennials have seen their mothers struggle to care for their kids while being in the labour market. Millennials are not naïve and they realize that the dream of having children, a life partner and a career might be challenging to achieve. Millennial men still face the pressure of being the breadwinner and providing for future families, while for women combining professional work with bringing up children is seen as a major challenge. In many cases, they do not think that their parents' lifestyles will suit their own, which leaves Millennials uncertain about how else to structure their lives. In an absence of clear guidance, many Millennials seem to prioritize their own enjoyment (Atwood & Scholtz, 2008).

The effects of individualization as the feeling of having to live your own life and being responsible for right and wrong choices can be found in the phenomenon of the quarter-life crisis. This crisis might reflect the tension between the promise of the 'world at their fingertips', when they feel that they can do and be anything they wish, and the awareness that much depends on luck and external circumstances. They are responsible for their decisions but feel they have little impact on how their decisions might turn out. Many Millennials are looking for guidance on how to structure their lives and in many cases they do not think that the template of previous generations will fit their own career and life. Due to a lack of alternative templates they search for new blueprints on which to model their life. This leads to rising anxiety and depression during those years.

PARADIGM SHIFTS AROUND WORK AND TECHNOLOGY

The workplace that the Millennials inherit will be different from the workplace that previous generations inhabited. The new workplace is no longer built around jobs for life and technology is paramount. The new workplaces are characterized by so-called boundaryless careers (Arthur & Rousseau, 1996). Boundaryless careers are mainly careers that move between different employers fairly seamlessly. Additionally, the term refers to the fact that traditional hierarchies of reporting and advancing are less important. Another element is that the marketability of one's skills is becoming more important, which means that the marketplace determines the value of individual labour power. This is often called an individualized form of labour, in which the individual operates like a small enterprise either within a traditional organization or as a self-employed person (Pongratz & Voß, 2003). While for previous generations these changes were taking place while they were in the workplace, Millennials are the first generation to enter a workplace that is characterized by boundaryless careers and individualized labour.

Research evidence on the changing structure of the labour market for Millennials is still scarce. To see real changes longitudinal research is required. However, some insights can be drawn from the employment experiences of previous generations. Academic research has indicated that the mean tenure and the percentage of people in long-term employment has fallen in the period from 1973–2006 in the USA (Farber, 2007). The research explored data from different birth cohorts from 1914–81, which means that only few Millennials were included. The research found that while men and women in their 20s change their jobs regularly, women in their 30s seem to stay longer in their jobs than men. This contributes to the overall trend that women in this research were more likely to be in long-term employment but the research did not offer any reasons as to why this might be the case.

While there is no data for the Millennial generation as of yet, there are two elements we need to keep in mind. First, it is known that younger people tend to try out different occupations and industries until they find jobs they like (Levenson, 2010). From a life cycle perspective younger individuals might 'test drive' some areas of work before deciding where the best fit for them is. Second, it has been argued that most of the changes in the labour market were driven by organizations rather than employees' preferences (Levenson, 2010). Organizations have become more flat and flexible in recent decades, which includes old hierarchies withering away and many people finding themselves on more flexible employment contracts or work schedules than before (Castells, 1996). These trends are driven by a new technological paradigm as well as globalization. Although there is not enough longitudinal data to make a judgement on whether or not job tenure has changed in the Millennial generation, it can be concluded that the changes are not necessarily driven by the wishes of the Millennial generation but by organizations themselves.

The two major tendencies dominating the changing labour market are a move from hours worked to output orientation and employability security. Traditionally an employer would buy, say, eight hours of labour from an individual (Pongratz & Voß, 2003). An employer could never be sure of the employee really producing the maximum he or she could in the time available. A more efficient system of organizing is to measure employees like one would measure a contractor: based on outputs. Instead of stipulating a certain number of hours of work per day, an employer would define certain outcome targets that the employee should achieve. This means that many employees now operate in similar ways to contractors and self-employed individuals who have to manage their own work based on externally set outputs and who have to market their skills continually through their network to find new employment if need be. If one stays with employers for shorter periods of time this means finding new jobs at regular intervals. This means that one has to position oneself towards to the market to ensure that other organizations will require one's skills and competencies. This has been called employability security (Kanter, 1995). Rather than having employment security, having employability security means that one remains employable with different organizations.

While the effects of the changing nature of labour for the Millennial generation have not been explored, it appears evident that the labour market that Millennials enter is fundamentally different from that of previous generations. It is now characterized by shorter tenure of employees and by the subsequent need of employees to retain employability security through continually marketing themselves through their networks. Employees now move between organizations more frequently and much of their work is organized on a self-managed basis. The burden of marketing oneself to remain employable now rests with the individual.

Apart from the perceived decline of jobs for life, another major trend that influenced this generation is technology. With the advent of the Internet, technology has changed many aspects of how we work and live. The arrival of the Internet is often compared in impact to the steam engine and the subsequent industrial revolution. However, in contrast to the industrial revolution, the digital revolution seems to be faster and more all-encompassing. Digital technology has spread incredibly quickly and now includes a great variety of people. This technical change will have a major impact on how Millennials experience life.

When we think about technology, we often follow a deterministic paradigm. We think that technology is created in a social vacuum. However, much research on science and technology has shown that technological development is in fact bound up with society (MacKenzie & Wajcman, 1999). This body of work has shown that technology is shaped by society and society shapes technology. Inventions are not made in isolation but inventors interact with a great variety of people, who influence the creation of new technology. While Steve Jobs for instance is often heralded as having transformed the world through the iMac, iPhone and iPad, he was able to spot good inventions and incorporate them into his products. While he is credited with having led the 'i' for Internet revolution, it is somehow ironic that Tim Berners-Lee, who is often credited with developing the central pillars of the world wide web, used one of Jobs's devices (a NeXT computer) to programme (Arthur, 2011). This is called the mutual shaping of technology and society and reminds us that technological and societal changes are intertwined.

When we try to think about Millennials it is evident that Millennials have 'grown up' with technologies like the Internet, the mobile phone and social networking. The Millennials grew up in times when those technologies matured and spread to the wider population. For many Millennials it will be difficult to understand how the world worked before the Internet. Their information search behaviour is now increasingly reliant on 'googling'. Rather than going through books in a library to find a definition of a term, they type it into Google or another search engine and are presented with a variety of potential answers that have to be evaluated for accuracy (the latter being one of the key challenges that Millennials have to understand). In order to connect to family and friends they are used to using a mobile phone for calling and texting. Millennials are also keen users of social networking sites like Facebook, which allows the sharing of personal information with so-called friends. While not all Millennials are hooked on technology, technology will shape the interactional patterns that Millennials display.

Those technologies will have a major impact on how Millennials interact. All those technologies allow some kind of immediacy and are fairly instant. Google will turn out the results for a search term almost instantly. On Facebook, just after posting a comment, many of your friends will interact with this content by posting a response or by clicking the 'like' button. Even with email, which is seen as a much slower way of communication, a reply can be expected within a period of time that tends to be much shorter than exchanging letters by 'snail mail' for instance. When Millennials call or text a friend on their mobile phone they can expect a response immediately or within a short time span. Being used to immediate interaction, this becomes a standard Millennials will expect in the workplace and in life more generally.

These two paradigm changes in relation to working practices and technology come together in the rise of importance of learning. In order to succeed in the workplace one has to learn constantly and for this it is vital to get feedback. The way that Millennials crave feedback will be constant and immediate, just like they experience it in technology. Millennials need to learn to keep their skills up-to-date to remain employable. It is in learning that the two paradigms shift as the loss of jobs for life and the technology paradigm come together.

A GENERATIONAL APPROACH TO LEADERSHIP DEVELOPMENT

One of the key challenges that emergences from the previous discussion is the fact that traditional leadership development has presumed that individuals will stay within an organization for long periods of time to develop individuals through the ranks until at one point they might be ready for leadership positions. With the changes in the labour market, an organization simply might not have the time to develop those leaders because Millennials leave the organization too early. With traditional leadership development only starting in earnest in the late 30s and 40s, this will be perceived as too late for many Millennials. Most organizations would talk about talent instead of leadership development in regard to Millennials but many Millennials feel that their ego is nourished better when seen as potential leader. This is a major problem for any leadership development activities in current organizations. Bringing the research discussed in this chapter together will constitute the next layer of the heuristic.

Let's start by looking at self-knowledge. First, *role models* continue to be important for Millennials. Millennials value authenticity and their role models therefore have to be authentic and have lived life based on their own values. The changing nature of careers also means that many role models will have achieved their success based on their own dedication and a good portion of luck. Millennials admire the ability to turn around one's life. Searching for authentic role models also means that standard role models will not be inspiring to individualized Millennials but those who are authentic and self-made will be. *Authenticity* not only plays a role for who Millennials admire

46

but it is centrally important when it comes to their own leadership development. Developing authenticity should be at the core of developing Millennials because it will fit well with their experience, which is shaped by individualization. Individualization means that Millennials feel unique and in control of their choices but they also know that consequences often depend on the external environment. This authenticity will be expressed in the Millennials' view on the private and public sphere. Organizations that allow Millennials to bring their private self to work will be seen as allowing for more authenticity but this authenticity can be at odds with perceptions of professionalism. This means not only that Millennials need to perceive senior leaders in the organization as authentic to emulate them but also that Millennials themselves need to develop their own authentic narratives to be perceived as leaders by others.

In a world of work in which Millennials are going to have to reinvent themselves several times throughout the course of their lives, acquiring knowledge is going to be central. *Experiental learning* can help Millennials to hone their leadership skills. For this generation regular feedback is incredibly important in honing their skills and remaining employable. It is therefore crucial to give Millennials regular and constructive feedback. In order to remain employable, Millennials also regularly need to top up their knowledge through *formal education*. MBA programmes and executive education programmes are going to remain crucial for this generation and many Millennials will also participate in specialist Masters degrees throughout their careers to reinvent themselves. In those formal education settings Millennials will experience an intense sense of community and their peers are going to be as important for their learning as their professors and reading material.

Developing social knowledge is also going to be crucial for Millennials. Millennials are self-confident and will want *visibility* early on in their careers. In fact many Millennials believe that they could do the job of a senior leader after the first half year. While this is clearly over-optimistic, having exposure to senior leaders will ensure that Millennials feel that their work is valued and important. Millennials should be given early responsibility by being asked to contribute to important projects in teams, which will feed their self-confidence without leaving them to their own devices. Leadership academies and working projects with senior leaders will therefore be important for developing Millennials. Another useful way of giving Millennials visibility is through strengthening their networking skills. Finally, the *organizational culture* has to be geared towards developing Millennials. It is important to pay Millennials well as remuneration is still more important to them than altruistic initiatives that allow them to give back to society. Work–life balance initiatives are vitally important for this generation, which values its leisure time. Millennials should be given time off and it might even work well to incentive them with additional holidays for good performance. For this organizations need to develop the right tools to manage the overflow of work into private life through technology.

By exploring how the research discussed earlier in this chapter affects leadership development, we were able to add an additional layer to our heuristic. This shows that considering Millennials in leadership development means changing the perspective of some activities. More details on the individual activities and the research underlying the insight will be provided in the empirically-based chapters that discuss each activity.

CONCLUSION

In this chapter we looked at the research evidence for generational changes and their implications for the workplace in general and leadership development specifically. The average Millennial can be characterized as confident, authentic, anxious (particularly in the face of ambiguity), assertive, money-driven, and lovers of leisure time and job security. Research on Millennials is rife with contradictions and apparent conflicts, and by drawing on sociological research on wider societal changes such as individualization, the end of job for life and technological changes, we were able to explain not only why these trait changes might have come about but also some of the apparent contradictions. These changes were considered in relation to leadership development for Millennials by adding an additional layer to the heuristic that indicates how leadership development needs to be altered so as to allow Millennials to grow.

4

MILLENNIAL WOMEN AS LEADERS

INTRODUCTION

After an event at which I presented this research on Millennials, I was approached by Anita, who said that my research resonated with her; it was exactly how she felt but she had never been able to express it in such a way. Anita grew up in South America, studied in the US and came to the UK for work. She is a typical go-getter. Excelling at school and university and then landing her dream job in a high profile consultancy. Yet all her education did not seem to have prepared her for her job. She did well in her career in a consultancy but not as well as she would have hoped. After several years in her current role she started to notice that her male peers suddenly advanced faster than she did – regardless of how hard she worked and how good her results were. Her cruel schedule meant that she had little private time and the constant travelling meant that she had few friends. She was asking herself what was the purpose of all this hard work. At 29, Anita decided to leave the consultancy job to do some spiritual travelling to 'find herself'. After a year of travelling in South East Asia, she decided that she wanted to return to South America to start her own company there.

This story is a fairly common experience for Millennial women. However, I found that many younger women struggle to make sense of their experiences and to see common patterns. This is probably why seeing the findings of my research strikes a cord with them; it offers them parameters to think through their own experiences. After exploring women's leadership development and Millennial leadership development in separate chapters, I would now like to bring both sides together to explore how particularly Millennial women can be developed as leaders. Here the power of intersectionality will be unfolded. I will be talking about professional women who are competitive and were educated within the paradigm that they can achieve everything they want. The chapter will start with a review of how gender is changing in the Millennial generation, to then discuss the decline in the male breadwinner model for Millennial women. I will then discuss the relationship of Millennial women to feminism as an explanation of their experience and the leadership potential of Millennial women. The chapter will conclude by providing the final layer of the heuristic to include Millennial women.

BLURRING GENDER

While many areas of academic research are rather obscure, gender is something on which everyone has an opinion. Such an engagement is welcomed but it also often means that we do not discuss research evidence but drift off into personal experiences that are not carefully reflected upon and analysed but taken as definite truths (you just have to think back to your last pub conversation on the gender differences that can be observed from an early age on in the daughter and son of your friend). In this section I will therefore offer my perspective on gender similarities and differences and gender change over time.

The nature-nurture debate has been held for a long period of time with some proponents arguing that gender differences are due to genetic differences while others have argued that they are due to socialization. Without rehearsing the argument here, it is important to state at this point that modern science agrees that gender is an outcome of not only biological make-up but also the environment. Leading research in the area has shown that many things we perceive to be biological are in fact malleable by society (for an excellent review of this, see Fine, 2010). While we believe that men and women are fundamentally different, meta-analyses find that few gender differences hold true across a range of studies (Hyde, 2005). Those meta-analyses compare the results of previous studies to find consistent patterns. Those that have been proven to be consistent differences are throwing velocity, throwing distance and physical aggression, but overall there is much more gender similarity than difference. If we just recur to biology to claim that we cannot change anything about gender, this ties our hands behind our back in creating change. Instead, it might be more fruitful to explore how gender constructions can be changed.

It is often argued in the popular media that women are the winners and men the losers of the knowledge economy. It is often shown that girls and women do better in school and university than their male counterparts (OECD, 2012). The argument of women's strong performance in education is regularly mobilized to argue that losing highly educated women means losing half of the talent pool, which in turn might affect organizational performance. The fact that women are doing better than men in education has led to calls that boys and men need special support to compete in the new economy.

However, we should not forget that women often are under-represented in science, engineering and technology education (OECD, 2012). While women do in fact seem to catch up and overtake men in education, stereotypes continue to shape their experience. There is for instance the stereotype that girls and women are not good at mathematics. Research has found that girls and women self-manipulate their maths performance by simply thinking that they ought to perform less good in mathematics. This is called stereotype threat (Roberson & Kulik, 2007). However, when one manipulates the experiments by having a woman administering the experiment, which is equated with being mathematical competence, or by having a sentence in the instructions stating that the test does not produce gender differentiated results, the gender differences in mathematics performance disappear. This is called stereotype reactance. Even though stereotypes can be manipulated in this way, it is important to recall that they often shape our behaviour and our performance – and also which areas we study.

Another often-recited reason is that the skills the knowledge economy needs, such as teamwork and customer service, are feminine. It is thereby presumed that women naturally have the better skillset to succeed in the knowledge economy. We can see that for instance in the rise in technology work of the hybrid worker who needs to have both social and technical skills (Woodfield, 2000). This often leads to the idea that women are the new ideal workers because they bring technical skills through their education and social skills as women. However, my research has indicated that it is men rather than women who continue to be seen as ideal workers because social skills are seen as normal in women and are therefore not regarded (and rewarded) as special (Kelan, 2008b). Men in contrast who have social skills are perceived as unusual because they are perceived as acting against their natural inclination and therefore are seen as a particularly suitable ideal technology worker. This indicates that how skills and merit are constructed is highly dependent on context. Sweeping assumptions about women as winners and men as losers of the knowledge economy are therefore too unspecific to help us understand gender at work.

While stereotypes influence our behaviour to a large degree, research has also evidenced a blurring of gendered traits. Cross-temporal meta-analyses on Millennials have shown that Millennial women are now more assertive than their female predecessors (Twenge & Campbell, 2008). This is only an indicator of a wider change in the appropriation of masculine and feminine values (Twenge, 1997). Psychological research has developed questionnaires to measure masculinity and femininity based on a range of attributes. Analysing the results of this research, it appears that women are now taking on more masculine attributes. In other words, Millennial women are becoming more like traditional men. But are Millennial men taking on more feminine traits as well? The answer is no. Millennial men are not adopting feminine traits. Women are increasingly displaying instrumental and assertive traits that were traditionally seen as the realm of men (Twenge, 2009). Instrumental traits include self-esteem, extraversion and narcissism as discussed earlier. However the counterpart to instrumental skills, the communal traits, which includes a regard for other people's feeling traditionally seen as feminine have not been re-valued. One can conclude from this that women are more open to adopting masculine traits whereas men are resistant to taking on feminine traits. In other words the parameter of what it means to be a woman has widened to include more masculine skills while the parameters of what it means to be a man have remained fairly static. It also shows that masculinity is probably more valued whereas femininity is less valued, which might explain why women gain status when adopting masculine traits whereas men lose status when adopting feminine traits.

It can therefore be argued that what we see is a continued evaluation of masculine attributes that are now adopted by women but no re-evaluation of feminine skills (Twenge, 2009). In fact, many approaches to developing girls and women focus on developing instrumental skills to teach them how to compete and make themselves heard. However, it has been neglected to teach men as well as women the importance of communal traits. It is exactly those communal traits that many jobs require now. If we for instance think about managers, a key requirement is that they develop others and for this communal skills are highly relevant. Yet in society overall they still seem to be devalued.

Rather than asking if gender difference is biological or social, a more useful approach seems to be to explore how gender expressed itself and how gender differences and similarities are interpreted. We have established in this section that much of our perception on gender difference is due to our own perceptions and assumptions or, as a well-known article has put it, 'believing is seeing' (Lorber, 1993). Gender is thus highly malleable by society.

THE DECLINE OF THE MALE BREADWINNER MODEL

This is an important insight that extends far beyond traits themselves. It is noticeable that women's lives have changed drastically in the last decades in Western countries, with more women going to university and being in paid employment (OECD, 2012). This challenges the traditional model of the male breadwinner and the female homemaker. It is important to remember that a pure breadwinner model never existed and women were always present in the labour market but never to the degree seen today (Lewis, 2001). This means in many cases there are equal breadwinners in the home or a woman might be the main breadwinner. My earlier research has for instance shown how the perception of risk is structured by whether or not a person is the breadwinner, and in this case the main breadwinner could be men or women (Kelan, 2008c).

An interesting US study has explored the effects of men's breadwinner status on their changing gender beliefs (Zuo, 1997). The study focuses on a 12-year period (1980–92) and uses relative breadwinner status in its research design. The men belonged to the Baby Boomer Generation and Generation X and were all married and remained married throughout the research period (the sample focused on heterosexual couples). Over the sample period most men showed an increase in gender egalitarian values, which was particularly prevalent with the younger participants. Men tended to agree that women should share the provider role but some traditional perspectives that saw women's roles mainly in the home whereas men's responsibility is to earn an income persisted. The research also highlights that most men still thought that they should earn more money than their spouses. While earlier parenting was mainly seen as a woman's role, in the study period it was observed that men took more responsibility for parenting. It was also found that men whose wives were near equal breadwinner had strong gender egalitarian views. This indicates that men's status as breadwinner has an impact on their views on gender. Although no similar studies exist for Millennials, the study is about the parents of the Millennials and is as such meaningful.

The perceived breadwinner role will come particularly under threat through boundaryless careers where spells of unemployment or underemployment are part and parcel of the employment experience. Research has explored how Baby Boomers and Generation X perceive unemployment when they have children (Forret, Sullivan & Mainiero, 2010). Again no similar studies on Millennials exist, mainly because many Millennials do not have children yet. However the research is nevertheless insightful when it comes to changing gender roles. This survey study found that men with children tend to see unemployment as a defeat whereas women with children tend to see unemployment as an opportunity to reinvent themselves. This suggests on the one hand that women are more readily able to adopt boundaryless career models but on the other hand it shows that the male breadwinner mentality is still enshrined in many people's minds. This is why unemployment for men with children is seen as more of a defeat than the same instance is for women. If men still carry the burden of being the breadwinner, losing one's job has serious implications for the identity of those men.

While the studies discussed earlier in this section related mainly to Baby Boomers and Generation X, there is a fascinating and extremely well-executed study that has explored young men and women in Germany (Allmendinger, 2009). The basis for the study is standardized interviews conducted in 2007 with 2,038 men and women belonging either to the 17 to 19 years or 27 to 29 years of age cohort. The same men and women were interviewed again two years later and 83% of the original number agreed to participate again. The interviewees were selected based on a complex quota system to ensure representation across different German states, educational attainment and employment status. This study explored men and women's perspectives on work and life.

Sociologically, we speak about a re-traditionalization of gender roles, which means that traditional patters emerge in a new dress (Adkins, 2000). This re-traditionalization can be observed mainly in Millennial men. The new guise of this re-traditionalization becomes visible in the fact that Millennial men in the German study used the modern language of wanting to take parental responsibility by taking paternity leave and spending time with their children, but they also saw themselves as the main breadwinner (Allmendinger, 2009). Only 7% of Millennial women saw their male partners as breadwinner and for them bringing up a family was seen as a shared responsibility. Men in contrast often saw themselves as breadwinner (20%). This clearly indicates gender differences in how men and women want to structure their lives: women want to live in egalitarian and dual-breadwinner constellations where their independence is important, whereas for men the traditional breadwinner role with a higher salary than their female partners, together with wanting to be an active parent, is the ideal. The gender differences also extended to money: while women saw it as a way to be independent, for men it meant power. Overall, Millennial women valued freedom and independence and wanted to combine a successful professional career with having a family. While Millennial women wanted modern arrangements with a shared breadwinner and caregiver status, Millennial men were more likely to favour re-traditionalized gender arrangements which meant being a breadwinner while being active fathers.

Research in the US came to similar conclusions. This research uncovered how Millennials conceptualize changes in regards to gender, family and working life through life-history interviews with 120 participants aged 18–32 drawn from a mix of socio-demographic backgrounds in the US (Gerson, 2002). In this research it became evident that the majority of individuals grew up in non-traditional households, which means that Millennials' parents were divorced, they grew up in single-parent households and their parents were working full-time. Having seen the arrangements in their parents' generation, for those Millennials partnerships have become more fluid, voluntary and indeed temporary, which means that new arrangements for paid work and care work need to be found. While there is a strong commitment to egalitarian gender views, the Millennials were aware of the fact that they are often difficult to achieve. This led to different second best options that were favoured by men and women. Men favoured an arrangement where they remain the breadwinner and women remain the primary carer. Women in contrast would prefer arrangements where they and their children are not economically dependent on men.

This divergence in life plans will have consequences for the workplace. If Millennial men see themselves in the role of provider, they will ensure that they get ahead in their career and increase their pay package. For women in contrast their pay package is mainly important in relation to maintaining their independence while bringing up children. This will lead to a mismatch in the long-run when men will suddenly move ahead in their jobs to gain better financial rewards and women might take the foot off the gas pedal to combine work and family. However, at this stage women will lack the tools to make sense of their experience, and it is this that I explore next.

MILLENNIAL WOMEN AND FEMINISM

Millennial women might see the world as their oyster. They have grown up in a world where many of the aims of second wave feminism have been achieved. The key demands for second wave feminism, which lasted from the early 1960s to the mid 1990s, were gender equality at work, at home and in society at large. An early precursor of the ideal worker that we have met in previous chapters can in fact be found in Simone de Beauvoir's seminal book *The Second Sex* (Beauvoir, 1949/1993), in which she argues that a male-centred ideology is accepted as the norm, ignoring the other (female) half of the population. Following this idea many second wave feminists fought inequality that was enshrined in the way societies were ideologically dominated by men. However, while for their grandmothers and mothers second wave feminism might have been a liberatory movement, for many Millennial women feminism seems to have lost its importance (McRobbie, 2008). However, it should be noted that the so-called third wave of feminism (examples include Walter, 1998; Baumgardner & Richards, 2000; Banyard, 2011) has offered some new ways of thinking through gender relations, which seem to resonate more with Millennial women.

A study showed that the young women had experiences of things which could be seen as reflecting gender inequality such as the difficulty in gaining respect, the lack of female managers, and earning less than male colleagues (Scharff, 2011a; 2012). The study consists of interviews with 40 women in the UK and Germany who were born between the late 1970s and late 1980s. This covers the older age group of the Millennials and the younger age groups of Generation X. Although these young women confronted gender inequality, rather than focusing on gender, they were happy to accept their age and lack of experience as reasons for their experiences. In addition, these young women stressed that they were individuals and were not thinking in the categories of men and women as structuring their experiences. This reflects the theory of individualization discussed earlier, which states that social conventions no longer bind individuals into their traditional roles and it is instead the role of the individual to succeed. Instead of seeing gender as an influential factor in their experience, these young women see themselves as agents who chose do to certain things while ignoring others. However, being an individual also means that there is little room for the collective identification and collective action that for instance feminism offered.

Furthermore it has been shown that women's rejection of feminism and feminists is in fact a way of constructing an identity as a young woman (Scharff, 2011b). In this study feminists were constructed by the young women in the study as unfeminine, man-hating and lesbian. Those identities were rejected by the young women. For these young women feminism was a movement that is passé and no longer required today. For those young women rejecting feminism was a way of constructing themselves as modern and liberated women who are in charge of their own life and rejecting feminism also meant rejecting non-heterosexuality (Scharff, 2011c) and a world in which gender matters. The preferred identities of these young women were feminine, man-loving and heterosexual.

From this discussion we can conclude that feminism is not something young women find attractive as a way to explain their experiences. Instead their experiences in the workplace are seen through the prism of them as individuals who are responsible for their own success and failures. This means that the rejection of feminism can be understood as a rejection of gender inequality as an important parameter to explain their experiences. These young women prefer to construct a world in which gender no longer matters and in which gender as the basis for different treatment no longer exists. However, by repudiating gender and stressing their individual power, they also lose any framework through which to think through the ways in which gendered structures still affect their lives. In part the rejection of feminism can therefore also be understood as a rejection of the idea that everything they experience is due to gender. However, rather than saying that some experiences might be related more to gender than others, younger women seem to disregard gender completely in order to appear as self-guided individuals.

As I have argued in regard to gender in general, this is a form of *gender fatigue* (Kelan, 2009a). This research looked at men and women of all age groups in the workplace and found that men and women are tired of constantly constructing a world where gender no longer matters in spite of evidence of the contrast. In other words, people are aware of the fact that gender might still play a role in the workplace, yet they have grown tired of trying to ignore gender in spite of this. This is a considerable effort and while most people would wish for a workplace where gender did not matter, the fact that gender still matters is hard to disguise. For young women this dilemma must be even more pronounced as they get the message in school and university that gender is no longer important and is therefore not talked about. To then be confronted with a workplace where gender still matters a great deal must come as a shock to those women, who never thought that their gender might disadvantage them.

MILLENNIAL WOMEN AND SELF-CONFIDENCE

It is regularly stated that women lack the self-confidence to be in top leadership positions and if women do not believe in themselves no one else will. This goes often hand in hand with the claim that women just do not want to have careers. It is interesting to note that a recent US study showed that Millennial women have overtaken Millennial men in their career aspirations (Patten & Parker, 2012). Millennial women now place more value on having a career than their male counterparts. This shows that may Millennial women want to succeed in their careers. The question is if they have the self-confidence to achieve this. While we know that the Millennial generation is in general more self-confident, it is worthwhile taking a closer look at gender differences in the Millennial generation in regard to self-confidence.

Millennial women are well educated but are they confident enough to become leaders? The previously discussed research in Germany found that half of the Millennial women have a better education than their mothers and 40% of the Millennial women have a better education than their fathers (Allmendinger, 2009). For men the gains in educational attainment were much lower. Women are well-educated but in the past it was often asserted that women lack confidence in themselves to become leaders. This was not sub-stantiated by the research, which showed that women had high self-confidence. As many as 99% of women describe themselves as good at what they do professionally. The research used images relating to sports and a fish shoal and asked the interviewees to position themselves as leaders. There was no difference in the percentage of men and women that picked leadership positions in those examples. There were no gender differences in regard to how men and women perceived their leadership skills: they saw themselves as communicative and efficient, appreciative of responsibility, able to get their views accepted and willing and able to give advice to others.

However women questioned themselves more. Millennial women indicated that they worried and were nervous more often than Millennial men. Women were also more often uncertain about appropriate types of behaviour. This might be related to the fact that women are more likely than men to perceive events as externally controlled. Whereas 44% of women indicated that if they confront difficulties, they question their own abilities, only 26% of men said the same. The research also indicated that competition is perceived as a motivation to a higher degree by men than women. This means that in spite of the fact that women show excellent performance and high leadership potential, they are insecure, question themselves more and shy away from competition more often than their male peers.

Millennial women also indicated that their performance was evaluated differently than that of men. Women saw their salary as not adequate and 90% of women and 80% of men agreed that the performance of women is evaluated differently to that of men. They also think that men are promoted more quickly than women. It is also notable that in the two years during which the research was conducted the percentage of women who believed that they could not achieve leadership positions grew from 19% to 27%. There was also a slight increase in the pessimism of men to reach the top, but from just 11% to 15%. Women thereby realize that they advance less quickly than men and are evaluated differently, which slowly eats away at their ambitions to become leaders.

Although the research does not trace the question of how women deal with the fact that, in spite of their abundant self-confidence, they will not climb the corporate ladder as quickly as men, it appears that exactly this conundrum is vital for understanding the decreasing motivation of younger women in the workplace. In other words, what happens if the self-confidence of young women is dampened by their male peers being promoted more quickly? Younger women will have never seen gender as much of a factor in their education and early work experience. If there are then confronted with a situation in which men are promoted more quickly, they will lack a framework by which to understand why this is the case and see the problem as residing in themselves. It is there that individualization will hit them hard because under individualization they feel responsible for their own success and failure even though they might realize that external forces guide success and failure. If young women do not draw on gender to explain their experiences, they are left with the impression that something must be wrong with them. They might feel that they not have done their job well or might not have worked on the important project, and so on. Over the long term this will increase women's dissatisfaction with their job and their life, particularly because they already feel that they are working incredibly hard and sacrificing other areas of their lives in order to achieve career success.

Women do not differ in their leadership potential and how they position themselves in competitive environments (Allmendinger, 2009). While Millennial women have leadership potential, they are nervous about their performance and career progress due to structural impediments. Women want to lead and can lead but Millennial women sometimes seem to have no faith that they can succeed in spite of these impediments. This is likely to be related to the fact that socialization teaches women to have self-doubt because this is a desired feminine quality. It appears that women sometimes seem to lack the self-confidence to go for it because they want to appear as feminine and the structural barriers just seem to hard to overcome.

DEVELOPING MILLENNIAL WOMEN AS LEADERS

In the previous two chapters we looked at leadership development from gender and generational perspectives. I would now like to bring the layers that explored gender and generation together by looking at the particular challenges and opportunities that might emerge from focusing on developing Millennial women as leaders. This will focus the area of concern and set us up to explore the different elements of the heuristic through the empirical material in the following chapters.

Self-knowledge first relates to *role models*. Role models are important because they provide identification. Millennial women are confronted with the problem that there are few senior women available to act as role models. In addition, the content of these role models often seems to be not right. *Authenticity* is not only key for Millennials but particularly important for Millennial women. It will also be important to stress that they can be whoever they want to be in the workplace but also to set realistic expectations of how that might look. It will be a particular challenge for women to be perceived as authentic leaders due to the masculine template of leadership.

Acquiring knowledge is going to mean that Millennial women need to be able to engage in *experiential learning*. Millennial women need to receive open feedback on their performance and need to be able to learn from this in order to transform their behaviour. The *formal education* that women can draw on to become leaders largely relates to doing an MBA degree. However, the elite MBA programmes are dominated by men, which means that women have to learn to survive in a minority position.

Finally, *social knowledge* relates to Millennial women gaining *visibility*. A traditional tool for developing visibility would be through women's networks, but with Millennial women's rejection of feminism, those might not be suited to developing women. The *organizational culture* might also not be conducive for Millennial women. Many Millennial women will realize that stereotypical assumptions influence their performance evaluation and thereby their potential to advance in organizations.

CONCLUSION

In this chapter we have analysed research on Millennial women and what this might mean for leadership development. While Millennial men and women share many traits and characteristics, it is evident that Millennial women in particular have started to adopt more masculine traits. However neither men nor women adopt more feminine skills. Exactly those feminine skills are crucially important for developing leaders who are not only technically competent and competitive but can also listen and empathize with their employees. While there is a decline in the male breadwinner mentality, this still seems to be a strong factor in many people's minds and in seeing who deserves a pay rise. While Millennial women have waved farewell to the male breadwinner model and want shared responsibility and financial independence, Millennial men seem to see themselves in the role of the provider for the family while being involved in bringing up their children. What distinguishes Millennial women from women of other generations is their attitude towards feminism. Millennial women often cannot connect to second wave feminism, which was the feminism of their mothers and grandmothers, and instead prefer to see a world in which gender does not matter and individualism reigns. While Millennial women believe in individualization and ignore gender, many of their experiences will only make sense through a gender lens. It is therefore important that junior women learn to understand when gender matters and when it does not. It is also notable that Millennial women have leadership potential and want leadership roles yet they are aware of structural impediments that might hinder their advancement. This might lead to Millennial women losing the motivation to be in senior roles. This poses some interesting challenges for developing not only Millennial women but also Millennial men for leadership roles. Using the final layer of the heuristic has highlighted the importance of intersectionality between gender and generations to fully understand how Millennial women can be developed as leaders. In the following chapters we will draw on empirical evidence to explore those challenges in greater detail.

5

ROLE MODELS — SEARCHING FOR THE IDEAL BUSINESS WOMAN

INTRODUCTION

Denise has a promising career in law ahead of her. Not only did she graduate top of her class, she also managed to land a job with one of the most esteemed law practices. She enjoys her work and she works extremely hard. When asked how she envisioned her future with the law practice, her normally confident speech became a bit quieter. Yes, she is keen to make partner. But – and this is a big BUT – she does not want to become like the female partners she has met. She calls them 'dragon ladies'. For her these dragon ladies are aggressive and more masculine than feminine. Denise feels that they 'sold out' on their femininity and are behaving just like men. In addition, only one of the three female partners in her law practice has children. And, as Denise adds, she has two or three nannies who care for them. The only time this female partner sees her children is early in the morning before she leaves for the office. By the time she returns the children are long in bed. Denise contemplates having children but she would also want to spend time with them. The other two female partners have failed marriages behind them and do not have a partner in their life. One of those female partners talks openly about how her marriage failed because she became too successful and her husband could not cope with that. None of these female partners seem to have any other interests outside work. Denise wants to have a challenging career and a fulfilling private life. And Denise does not want to be a dragon lady.

This narrative is interesting from a variety of perspective. First, it shows how important role models are. Second, it indicates how women often relate to one another in the workplace. In this chapter, we will trace how Millennial women relate to role models and how gender is important to this process. Based on this analysis and the insights that role models are important for leadership development, we will then make suggestions about how role modelling can be reshaped to allow Millennial women and men to develop an array of role models. The chapter will thereby explore the first dimension that was singled out as important for leadership development, role models, which forms parts of the self-knowledge element of the heuristic.

GENDERED IDENTIFICATION AT WORK

One of the most common reasons cited for the lack of female leaders is that there are just not enough role models for women (Kilian, Hukai & McCarty, 2005; Ibarra, Carter & Silva, 2010). This leads to a bit of a chicken and egg problem. There are few women in leadership positions and there are not going to be more because they lack role models. As a circular argument this is not particularly helpful when it comes to changing the situation. However, it does not seem to be only the scarcity of female role models that women complain about. Many women also complain about the fact that the female role models they are presented with are somehow not right for them. Being female is obviously only one axis based on which identification can happen, but given that it is considered an important one it is worthwhile exploring this further. Before we trace this dynamic, it is worth including some more theories on role models and related concepts.

Role models are essential for leadership development because they show the aspiring leaders their potential selves. On the most basic level a role model is a way of identifying. Let's first differentiate role models from mentors. Mentoring usually is seen as requiring consent from the mentor to engage in an interactive relationship in which being a role model can emerge as part of the interaction (Ragins & Cotton, 1999). Mentors are often assigned as part of a formal mentoring programme. Role model relationships can be much more distant, and in fact one-sided. One can for instance have a person as a role model without even having met a role model in person. In recent time, there is also much talk about sponsoring for women. While mentoring relationships can evolve on any hierarchical level, sponsorship relationships imply a more senior sponsor who promotes the protégée and thereby advances him or her. In fact research surveying men and women in the workplace found that women have more mentoring relationships than men (Ibarra, Carter & Silva, 2010). A mentor helps navigate organizational politics and increases the mentee's sense of self-confidence through developmental feedback. While a mentor is often assigned or agrees to mentor someone else, a sponsor has to be earned. The fact that sponsorship is earned makes it much more difficult to create programmes where a sponsor is assigned a protégée. A sponsor will put his or her reputation on the line for the protégée, which means that the sponsor must be convinced of the protégée's ability. Interestingly, research shows that men have more sponsoring relationships than women (Ibarra, Carter & Silva, 2010). The sponsor gives the protégée visibility as well as developmental assignments. They also fight for the protégée to ensure that she or he is promoted. Given the fact that sponsoring relationships not only provide candid advice but also advocate for the protégée, this research suggests that women advance less quickly than men because of the lack of sponsorship.

So why are these relationships important? Role models, sponsors and mentors can all provide ways of identification. Identification allows individuals to reshape their identity by comparing it to the identity of others, playing with those identities and eventually adopting others derived from this identification. Role models are a way of establishing identification. Identification can unfold in two forms: admiration and idealization (Sandell, 1993). Admiration means that one finds a person one identifies with and appreciates this person in a critical way, which means that one admires some aspects of that person but not the person in their entirety. Idealization, by contrast, involves an exaggeration beyond realistic merits. Admiration is in a sense more realistic. Admiration and idealization are therefore subcategories of identification where idealization contains an unrealistic aggrandizement of another person and admiration does not. We will return to this definition later on.

Research has suggested that individuals often identify with others who are similar to themselves, and gender and race are often used as categories for this shared similarity (Quimby & DeSantis, 2006). This explains why women often look for other women as role models. However, due to the scarcity of senior women in their immediate environment they might have to look further afield. Moreover, when we talk about mentoring, which generally requires a personal relationship to the person, the scarcity of senior women has another consequence: senior women will be overburdened with requests to act as mentors for more junior women.

The gender dynamics of role models are currently under-researched and the vignette with which this chapter opens shows that it is often not only the number of female role models that is problematic but also the content of the identification. As the example of Denise shows, such relationships among junior and senior women might not be without problems. Millennial women often seem to want to see role models who have a successful professional and private life and who juggle their different demands seamlessly. However few senior women around them seem to fulfil this requirement because they have made choices that Millennial women do not want to make.

In the research there is much debate about the Queen Bee syndrome, which might explain why junior women struggle to identify with more senior women. The Queen Bee syndrome presumes that women are in competition with one another. In the workplace that means being in competition for a limited number of senior roles that are implicitly reserved for women. It has, for instance, been shown that female faculty would assess the motivation of women studying science and engineering subjects lower than that of their male peers (Ellemers et al., 2004). The researchers interpret this as meaning that women on the science and engineering faculty want to retain their token status and to disassociate themselves from other women. Those female faculty want to be the exception to the rule and do not want to have other women following them who might diminish their status and achievement. Like women in senior business roles, it might be the case that those few women in science and engineering who 'made it' against the odds believe that those women who come after them should do the same.

However, the Queen Bee syndrome is heavily contested by academics, who argue that it ignores the complex and multifaceted relationships that women have in the workplace (Mavin, 2008). The Queen Bee syndrome, for instance, ignores the fact that senior women might be overwhelmed by requests to be the main female role model who is requested to represent the company's openness in regard to gender on every occasion. One aspect of this is that senior women themselves might realize that they are not an ideal businesswoman and have made certain choices in their careers that they think junior women might not approve of. A senior woman might, for instance, have decided not to have children or she might have someone at home who manages their private life. This can be a nanny, but for many senior women it might also be husband whose main role it is to keep the family going. Senior women might perceive themselves as less good role models because they realize that they cannot have it all and that there are compromises they had to make in the course of their journey to the top. They might feel that the junior women judge them for those choices.

Another explanation for the fact that many Millennial women cannot find role models seems to relate to the ideal worker norm. Women in management positions generally have to comply with an ideal worker who is described based on masculinity. In other words, one has to be masculine in order to be manager. Researchers have called this the 'think manager – think male' phenomenon. Research has shown that business students perceive the successful middle manager as more masculine, which means that they have more of the characteristics and attitudes that are commonly associated with men than with women (Schein et al., 1996). This was the case in the US, the UK, Germany, Japan and China, which speaks for the fact that the masculine ideal of a manager permeates different cultures. This means that in order to fulfil the masculine template of a manager, many women have to perform masculinity. At the same time women also need to appear feminine so as to count as women. This means that women can appear too feminine, while too much masculinity makes them appear in conflict with their gender role. This is commonly called the double bind for women in leadership positions (Gherardi & Poggio, 2001). The perception that women leaders are too harsh or threatening – just think of the connotations of 'ball breaker' or 'queen bitch' – might be due to the fact that they enact the masculinity required from their job which may be at odds with their femininity.

We often presume that having a role model leads to a kind of mimesis. Mimesis is the imitation of another person, meaning that people become 'mini-me' versions of the person they identify with. As a strategy this might be less effective both for the individual as well as the organization. If ideal workers are just reproduced in organizations this means that the same template is used over and over. The organization is not only missing out on diversity but also on the influx of new ideas and concepts that people who do not fit the template might bring. At the same time, individuals have to conform to a narrow band of acceptable behaviour lived by the role model. This is particularly problematic in regard to gender because many women will fall short of the ideal businesswoman who has a successful career, time for her children and a caring husband. This disallows any individuality that people might bring to the workplace and will counteract the needs of Millennials to be authentic.

In this section we have reviewed some of the literature on role models, sponsors and mentors from a gender perspective. This will function as a backdrop to the next section, where we will explore how these types of behaviour were manifest in some of the interviews. A particular focus will be on the differences between idealization and admiration where idealization includes an unrealistic aggrandizement whereas admiration does not. It will be argued that admiration is therefore more realistic because it includes a more realistic assessment of the other person. In addition, it facilitates the construction of composite identities that contain elements that are considered useful by a variety of people.

IDEALIZATION – IDEAL LEADERS AS ROLE MODELS

We have often presumed that the Organization Man, who was loyal to his organization and could in return expect long-term employment, is dead and replaced by a new persona that is not only gender neutral but ideally suited to displaying the key skills, such as flexibility and authenticity, needed to succeed in the new economic formation. This is the new ideal worker. In our research we did indeed detect a new kind of person that was eulogized by many people. This person was self-made and either the founder of an organization or a CEO. Often these people were authentic and charismatic, which added to the appeal of idealizing them.

Being 'self-made' was one of the characteristics regularly alluded to when Millennials discussed who they admired. Matthieu, for instance, who is originally from France, talked about a former colleague of his as a person he admired because he 'started from zero and definitely became somebody'. Another example is Ganesh, who is from India and has come to study in London. He quotes his father as a person he admires. His father came from a migrant family and the family set up a small business. His father then grew the business significantly into a regional and national market leader, and it is Ganesh's ambition to now take the family business to a global level. What he admires about his father is that he is a first generation entrepreneur who built the business from nothing into a recognized market leader. The ambition of Ganesh is now to grow the business internationally, which is why he thought that studying business in London would be an ideal way to explore how he can do this.

A similar narrative of coming from nothing to become someone was recounted by Luke. Luke is British and had an already illustrious career that would look great on a person a decade or two older than him. Luke gave us a whole range of persons he admired, but I would like to focus first on one who shared the self-made nature of the other examples. One of the persons Luke identifies with comes from poor background, but he was good at sports and was able to attend a fee-paying school on a scholarship. After school, this person set up a car dealership, which led to great wealth by the time he was 50. With his spare cash the person set up a racing team, which was one of his long-term dreams and apparently also a lucrative endeavour. For Luke the fact that this person is self-made is very important. Additionally, he also liked the ethical integrity of this person and that this person was true to his values, which is an expression of authenticity.

The first three examples we used all came from men and identified with men. Another great example of the self-made narrative becomes from Peggy. She has a lot of respect for Oprah Winfrey. She describes Oprah Winfrey as coming from a very poor background in which education was not valued. However she did not let this poor background stop her from making herself successful. For Peggy that is the quintessential American dream and she acknowledges that something like this would not be happen in Europe or Canada (she is from Canada originally). What she admires here is the ability of Oprah Winfrey to turn her life around and to make herself extremely successful (which in modern show business comes also with a bank balance to match). Overcoming adversity is one of the elements that Peggy admires.

Another example of a woman identifying with another woman is Frances. Frances talked about Anita Roddick as inspiring her. The founder of the Body Shop is described as incredibly successful while having stuck to her principles. Frances describes that Anita Roddick was never forced to fit into someone else's mould but instead set up a business that fitted her own belief system. What comes through in this account is the fact that Anita Roddick was authentic and stuck to her ideals instead of fitting into a predetermined template. She was able to do this because she created her own business environment by setting up her own company. It appears that authenticity and being true to yourself are key to success.

One of my favourite examples is from Emma. Emma had a privileged upbringing and lived in many countries during her childhood of which only part was spent in her native USA. Emma decided to work in consultancy before doing an MBA. After completing her MBA she continued to work in consultancy. Her choice of an admired person was Mireille Guiliano, who is the author of books such as *Why French Women Don't get Fat*. Mireille Guiliano was born in France but then moved to the US, where made a career in the wine and spirits and luxury goods industry. What Emma admires in Mireille Guiliano, whom she met when she gave a keynote, is not only her elegance but also her ability to be successful in business without turning into a man. In the case of Mireille Guiliano this is wrapped in the stereotype of the French woman, who is sophisticated, stylish and slim, yet enjoys her life (food in particular) while being very successful in her job. Originally trained as an interpreter, Mireille Guiliano has transformed her life, becoming not only a successful businesswoman in general but also a female entrepreneur.

She is self-made, too. Mireille Guiliano offers her own answer to the double bind, which seems to be appealing to Emma.

What struck me when analysing the interviews is the fact that many Millennials seem to have a deep idealization for people who made it under their own steam. Those self-made people, which includes the normal suspects such as Richard Branson and Steve Jobs, are used as ideals for Millennials. Most of these idealized personalities had to overcome some kind of hardship before they became successful. They also stuck to their guns. Instead of the transformation into someone else when at work, we here see that authenticity and being true to one's values are central. This ability to be oneself yet to be successful in business and life are the treasured and idealized values of Millennials. Interestingly, these idealized role models did not necessarily seem to contain a gender dimension. Both men and women are idealized.

ADMIRATION – THE ADMIRED SENIOR WOMAN

Overall, we noticed that all men selected men as their role models. Women had more diversity in their selection of role models: they selected men or women or both men and women. While this is interesting in its own right, it is even more fascinating to see that women also tended to identify with their female role models differently by using admiration rather than idealization. While we observed that men and women idealized other men and women, we found that admiration was more typical for women describing other women. We also found that some of the self-identified gay men in the research used similar patterns of identification and tended to describe their role models through admiration, which included more ambivalence.

Let's start by talking a look at how Dawn talks about the person she identified with. Dawn's role model is a woman who is described as one of the few in their mid-50s to work in back-end database programming, which is the most technical end of programming. What Dawn finds unusual about her role model is that she persisted with working in this technical position and has done so for more than 20 years. Dawn describes this as very unusual because it is rare to see a woman working for a long time in such a technical area of programming. While Dawn's role model belongs to the rare breed of women in technical jobs, Dawn also observes that her role model's emotions often come through in business. For Dawn that is not necessarily a good thing. Showing agitation or being frustrated in a business meeting is something that for Dawn is not professional. However, she offers the explanation that her role model is just very invested in the business. This passion for one's job is for Dawn generally a positive thing, but she thinks that to be a professional one has to be more reserved and not allow your emotions to shine through.

Talking about emotions is obviously a gendered topic. Women are often perceived as being more expressive and as showing their emotions more. However, the ideal worker is fairly emotionless and more instrumental in 'his' orientation. What we see here is an interplay between presumed feminine skills of expressiveness and presumed masculine skills of instrumentality. The masculine skills are equated with what it means to be successful in business, which is probably why Dawn feels ambivalent about her role model showing emotions at work. Her role model departs from the masculine norm of the instrumental and unexpressive ideal worker and this causes Dawn some discomfort, who says that showing emotion is not necessarily something that she aspires to.

Frances' idealization of Anita Roddick has been discussed already. Her response shows us that many accounts do not fall neatly into either admiration or idealization but oscillate between the two ways of describing role models. After Frances talked about how Anita Roddick was true to her values, which speaks for her authenticity, she voiced some doubts as to whether or not Anita Roddick was indeed authentic. Frances describes how she once suspected Anita Roddick of being a bit of a fraud. She thereby implies that Anita Roddick is less authentic but instead plays the role of being a successful business owner who believes in alternative ways of doing business but in the end might just be a regular business owner with no special values. However, Frances says this doubt was wiped away when she heard Anita Roddick speak. She experienced her as very open about her business, herself and her values, which was for Frances in line with how she wanted to perceive Anita Roddick. While Frances had these nagging doubts about Anita Roddick, she was able to transform her admiration, which included some ambivalence, and convert it into idealization, in which all the skills, traits and behaviours are aggrandized.

This shift from idealization to admiration is often very subtle, as the example of Frances shows. Another of such example comes from Caroline. Caroline talks about her female role model, an academic turned political adviser, whom she describes as very female and almost girly. This endorses her status as a woman by showing her femininity. At the same time her role model is a strongly minded woman who knows what she wants and how to get it. She is also very competent and knows what she is talking about. Frances admires

70

the entire poise that her role model builds around her. What we see in this account is a combination of masculine and feminine skills in a female role model. While the role model is described as very much a woman, at the same time she is also competent and knowledgeable, which are more instrumental skills that are often ascribed to men. Caroline's role model combines these two gendered characteristics and thereby bolsters her feminine identity as well as her masculine knowledge of the subject. Like many senior women, this role model is able to transcend the contradictions between masculine and feminine skills and the traditional double bind women in leadership positions find themselves in. Rather than just aggrandizing the role model, the role model appears realistic and shows a variety of traits.

We encountered such constructions a great deal when female role models were described and it can also be traced in Helen's role model. Helen's role model is a woman who set up a chocolate business and has a reputation of anarchy in the industry. She left the company she set up under a cloud, which is described by Helen as something she admires because her role model then went on to create another business that today is very successful. While being seeing as an anarchist in the industry and leaving one's own company under a cloud often might not be positive characteristics for Helen, this makes her role model more real and in a sense more authentic. Particularly because she went on to set up another successful venture. Apart from her successful business Helen continues 'But she also has a family and children and so she seems to have a good balance'. This suggests that for women to be complete they need a family and children and this balance in life is central. The 'but' Helen uses indicates a turning point in how the narrative is constructed. What we see here is how the professional self of having a successful yet controversial career is combined with having a successful private life, too. At the same time Helen is not sure that her role model really has a good balance because she does not know her. This suggests that maybe this is just a facade that her role model built up and in reality her private life might not be picture perfect. As in the previous example we see that here female role models have to combine a variety of behaviours that not only span masculinity and femininity but also the public and private life.

This is confirmed by Ulrike's statement, who talks about her aunt in her native Germany as her role model. Her aunt was very successful not only in her job but also a mother who is available for her children. This suggests that often women who are successful in business might be mothers but that they are not available for their children. What becomes clear here is that being a businesswoman and having children is seen for many women as difficult. It is an issue that they see as relevant for their future life and they seem to recognize that 'having it all' could be an issue but could also be entirely possible in their view.

What becomes apparent in those statements is that the idealizations of the authentic, self-made CEO and founder featuring in the idealization narratives was more complex and multi-layered in some cases, mainly when women discussed their female role models. This can be called admiration, which is more realistic and is less aggrandizing of the role model. For female role models admiration was more often chosen because they do not fit neatly into the ideal worker template, which in this case is characterized by being self-made and authentic but also by being more masculine than feminine and being more in the public than the private sphere. This ideal worker did not work for many women when looking for a role model as their role model did not only have to be an ideal worker, they also had to be an ideal businesswoman.

This ideal businesswoman transcends masculinity and femininity and combines her public and private self effortlessly. These ideal businesswomen not only show masculinity to appear as an ideal businessperson, but also combine it with femininity to bolster their identities as women. They also have to be successful in their career, while at the same time not only having a family but also having time for the family. The Millennial women therefore created for themselves an alternative role model to the self-made, authentic CEO and founder that was often idealized. This role model was the ideal businesswoman combining masculine and feminine skills while being successful at work and in her private life.

Yet many of the Millennial women voiced some ambivalence towards these ideal businesswomen. They suspected that they might be frauds and they suspected that their family life might not be as ideal as they portray it. These women showed more ambivalence and this ambivalence means that that the ideal businesswoman does not appear idealized (and aggrandized), but rather admired. However, with this admiration comes a more realistic expectation of what their female role models might look like.

In those accounts of Millennial women, it became clear that they would face some of the challenges of being ideal businesswomen in the future and they were realistic about what this entails. It also became clear that ideal businesswomen have to offer more than the ideal worker because they have to be successful in both their public and private lives and have to combine masculine and feminine skills.

COMPOSITE ROLE MODELS AND NEW
MENTORING CONNECTIONS

From a leadership development perspective, having role models, mentors and sponsors is important because it allows people to explore potential leadership identities. The lack of female role models is one of the most commonly quoted hindrances to the progress of junior women. However, we have highlighted in this chapter that it is not only the numerical availability of senior women that is a challenge for the identification of Millennial women with their potential selves, but furthermore the content of the role models that seems to create different identification patterns for Millennial women. While the authentic, self-made CEO and founder is the idealized and aggrandized role model of many Millennials, Millennial women often admired a businesswoman who has combined a successful private and professional life. The businesswoman had to combine a successful private life with a career, and masculine with feminine types of behaviour. This causes some friction and conflict in the narratives, but most Millennial women acknowledged that being a businesswoman might entail combining different elements. In fact, the businesswoman became more realistic through being admired rather than idealized.

However being a businesswoman and perfect on all accounts is a tall order and this is why in reality many senior women fall short of this admiration. It is not surprising that for many Millennial women the choices that more senior women have made do not appear as right. All too often they decided not to have children, are divorced or have 'outsourced' their children. What these young women confront here is the fact that workplaces were designed for the ideal worker, who is masculine and has a wife at home who takes care of the private life. Workplaces today have not changed enough to allow a great multitude of ideal workers. This is why the ideal worker still differs from the businesswoman that Millennial women are looking for.

How can organizations help Millennial women to develop role models? First of all, while Millennial women might find a female role model they admire, all too often real women fall short of their requirements. Instead it might be useful for Millennial women and indeed men to think about developing composite role models. Rather than having a role model that they completely idealize, Millennials might want to create composite role models of skills, attributes and behaviours they admire in individual people. They should learn that they can take certain characteristics from each of them without needing to emulate their complete identities. Millennial women should not only look for women as their role models but should rather draw their role models from a variety of sources and build their own 'composite role models' containing skills, behaviours and attributes they want to include in their identities. In fact Millennial women are closer to this than Millennial men because they split their role models into different attributes and behaviours, of which they admire some but not all. This might take some pressure off Millennials to find just one role model.

Second, it was interesting to notice that Millennial men did not mention female role models. To be clear, these Millennial men might have female role models but they did not mention them in the interviews. Although it is difficult to speculate why this is the case, one might want to suggest that this reflects an ideal worker who is still more male than female. We have seen when we reviewed the literature on masculine and feminine traits from a generational perspective that women have adopted masculine traits but men have not adopted feminine traits. For Millennial men it might therefore be important to connect with role models that exhibit these feminine traits. While not necessarily only women, encouraging men to find female role models might be a step to re-value feminine skills. It might also help to raise more awareness for gender issues in the work context that Millennial men are not aware of. It could for instance be explored in how far senior women could mentor Millennial men to sensitize them towards gender in the workplace and to develop men as inclusive leaders. Such a formal mentoring programme might help lead to a change in role models.

Speaking more generally about awareness for gender, mentoring programmes have an important role to play here. While traditionally junior women would be mentored by senior women, women would also profit from being mentored by senior men. Millennial women would be able to learn from senior men and senior men in turn would gain a better understanding of what it means to be a woman in leadership. This would raise awareness of gender for senior leaders and might even lead to a sponsoring relationship. This also means that the few senior women will not be overburdened by being a mentor to many junior women and in addition senior men would increase their awareness of gender in the workplace. This might have a wider knock-on effect than just identification because it might lead to other changes such as a more flexible notion of how an ideal worker might look and how life and work are integrated.

SIGNATURE PRACTICE: ACHIEVING BALANCED LEADERSHIP THROUGH RECIPROCAL MENTORING

Aviva, the British multinational insurance company, has taken a holistic approach to diversity and inclusion in leadership development through its balanced leadership initiative. This initiative set out to achieve a balanced pipeline for future leaders in regards to gender and other dimensions of diversity. Currently 20% of senior leaders at Aviva are women, which compares favourably with other financial service organizations. However, Marie Sigsworth, Group Corporate Social Responsibility Director at Aviva says that this is 'not enough' for them. One of the initiatives that Aviva launched as part of the balanced leadership initiative was a reciprocal mentoring programme. The programme started in June 2011 and included ten women and one gay man, all of whom were mentored by the 11 members of the executive committee. The mentees were selected based on their leadership potential with special attention was paid to diversity in regard to gender, cultural background, role in the organization, sexuality and location. While this was not a programme specifically designed for Millennials, it contained the older cohort of Millennials, with many mentees being in their 30s. The mentees meet their mentors once every two months in an informal setting that allows for an open exchange.

Even though this is only a small programme, its effects are immense. First, the mentees feel valued and receive important advice on their career development. Second, the mentors learn about the challenges that diverse potential leaders face at Aviva and what might hold them back. This led to many 'light bulb' moments where the executives realize their own privilege in achieving their positions and why others might struggle to do likewise. The experiences of the reciprocal mentoring programme have led the Chief Information Officer (CIO) for instance to start group discussions on the situation of women in information technology (IT). Overall, the reciprocal mentoring program raises awareness for gender and diversity at the top level. The tone from the top is important to re-shaping the organization to allow diverse people to take leadership positions.

Rather than following an approach whereby women mentor other women or whereby the pairings come from the same school of thought, Aviva matched people with different backgrounds and perspectives. This increases the challenges of the mentoring relationships, in which the mentor not only imparts advice but also learns from those who he or she might not otherwise listen to. The effects of the reciprocal mentoring programme meant that debates around diversity were re-energized and re-focused. In concert with other activities, the reciprocal mentoring programme has led to an improvement in succession planning processes to ensure that a stronger and broader pipeline for diverse talent is built for senior management roles. An approach similar to reciprocal mentoring practised by Aviva could help Millennial women see people they can identify with to build their composite role models. As a matter of fact, Aviva plans to broaden the program by including a specific focus on generational differences in the future. This would speak to the Millennial generation because they would not only get advise from more senior people in the organization but they would also would feel that their opinion is valued and taken into consideration.

In contrast, sponsoring is more difficult to tackle as sponsors are earned and not just assigned. The sponsor puts his or her reputation on the line to fight for their protégée in important meetings and their developmental opportunities. These sponsoring relationships have existed for a number of years as favouritism, which often includes the ideal of sponsoring a person who looks more like us. However, this template and mini-me mentality is not suitable for ensuring that talent is well used in organizations. A wider change in organizational culture and individual perception is required. Awareness training for senior and middle level managers can have a great effect here. More importantly, however, Millennial women need to realize how they can gain a sponsor by finding the right balance between good performance and visibility in the organization. We will explore this in greater detail in the following chapters.

SIGNATURE PRACTICE: ENCOURAGING A MULTIPLICITY OF SPONSORING RELATIONSHIPS

While nourishing an internal network of sponsors is central for Millennial women, a key question is what happens to these relationships if sponsors leave the organization. This is a particularly pressing issue in emerging markets like India, where the demand for talent is high. If a sponsor leaves the organization, women may lose an internal supporter as well as the prospect of progressing in the company. It is therefore particularly important that women develop multiple sponsors and advocates in the organization. This is exactly what the global American Express sponsorship program seeks to achieve. American Express sees sponsorship as a critical relationship that must be earned rather than something that is assigned. This means that men and women need to understand the importance of sponsor relationships and how they are cultivated, nurtured and sustained over time.

American Express piloted its 'Pathways to Sponsorship' program for a cohort of high performing, high potential women in the UK and the US (Opportunity Now, 2011). It is part of a broader initiative at American Express called 'Women in the Pipeline and at the Top', which is focused on the advancement of women into senior roles in the organization and on creating a more gender inclusive culture. The 'Pathways to Sponsorship' programme identifies potential senior female leaders and provides them with a customized development programme and structured approach to building key relationships within the organization.

After piloting the sponsorship programme in the US, UK and most recently Australia, American Express prepared to launch it in India. The programme aims to support senior women leaders in American Express India in developing and strengthening sponsorship relationships. Before the programme could be implemented, it was important to ensure that the organizational culture was ready for this approach and that leaders would support it. This was achieved by ensuring that leaders fully understood the role of sponsorship in professional growth and by forging partnerships with the Women's Interest Network (WIN) and broader diversity and inclusion initiatives in India. Sponsor Effect workshops were also conducted for female and male employees to increase awareness of both the importance of sponsorship and of having a network of sponsors. The sponsorship programme in India incorporates the insights from the pilot programmes. This includes encouraging women to take greater ownership in building a network of sponsors to ensure that when people move on, these aspiring female leaders will continue to have internal sponsorship. Having a multiplicity of sponsoring relationships thus ensures that high potential women can draw on internal support to advance their careers.

CONCLUSION

While Millennial women should create their own version of them-selves, rather than emulate others, it is important that they have role models, mentors and sponsors that can inspire them. The lack of available female role models is often cited as a major impediment for developing women as leaders. In this chapter we have seen that it is not only the numerical scarcity of women that is problematic but furthermore the content of these role models is different. We have seen that the idealized role model for Millennials is the authen-tic, self-made CEO leader, who were aggrandized. When female role models were talked about they tended to be admired, which means that skills, attributes and behaviour were more critically discussed and only accepted partially. This was the case because the ideal leader is still perceived as more of a man than a woman. Women were therefore looking for alternative role models who combine a successful professional life with a successful private life. Such perceptions of role models are more realistic because they avoid the aggrandizement of an idealized role model. It was argued that this can be taken even further by encouraging Millennial women to develop composite role models through which they combine behav-iours and traits from multiple persons. This is a model not only for Millennial women but also for Millennial men, whose role model identifications are still very traditional. This means for instance encouraging Millennial men to identify with senior women. This might be helped through a mentoring programme in which senior women mentor Millennial men. This would raise the gender aware-ness of Millennial men and would slowly change the ideal leader model used. A major challenge remains that senior female leaders are often burdened with a lot of mentoring for junior women and adding junior men to this might just prove too challenging. It would therefore help if senior men took a leading role in mentoring junior women. This would also raise awareness in senior men about gender issues and might just help junior women to develop spon-soring relationships. Now we have looked at the first element of self-knowledge, the next chapter will explore the second dimension, authenticity.

6

AUTHENTICITY — TELLING YOUR OWN STORY

INTRODUCTION

When Anton joined the Internet bank where he currently works, he loved the fact that his employer seems to support individuals in being themselves at work. Before joining the Internet bank, Anton completed an apprenticeship in banking in Germany before achieved a dual degree that involved studying and working at the same time. After he finished his studies, Anton looked for a bank that would allow him to bring more of himself into his work. After being made an offer by an Internet bank he did not hesitate but took the job. He was attracted by the fact that most customer contact is online and over the phone and he no longer had to wear a suit to work. He liked the first months and felt happy in the organization, but one day, he was called into the office of his manager. The manager was fuming. Anton had regularly updated his Facebook status and as Facebook was not blocked in the office he presumed that his employer allowed Facebook usage. When updating his Facebook status, he sometimes made comments about clients, which included messages about how happy he was to serve them but also sometimes messages on their unreasonable requests. His manager had a list of his Facebook status updates printed out in front of him, of which some were highlighted. His manager told him that it was unacceptable to talk about his work on social media sites like Facebook. Anton did not understand. He thought that using Facebook was his private endeavour and he made sure only to update Facebook in his lunch break and not during working time. None of clients were his 'friends' on Facebook. However, the company view was that no business-related matter was to be discussed outside of the company, which included any discussions on Facebook. Anton had apparently misjudged the informality of the workplace. While the online bank encouraged him to be himself at work, this authenticity apparently did not translate to his social media use.

Anton's experience is fairly typical for the older cohort of Millennials, who often wish to express their authenticity through social media. Being authentic is also a major topic in leadership development, where authentic leaders are seen as those who live their values and through this inspire others to follow them. This is often done through telling one's own story, which is academically often called a narrative. Being authentic requires an individual to blur the distinction between private and public spheres. However, for women, being authentic leaders is often regarded as challenging due to the double bind: if women are being leaders, they are seen as inauthentic in relation to their gender identity; if they are being feminine, they are seen as inauthentic leaders. In this chapter we take a look at how Millennials think about authenticity in relation to social media and what this means for developing Millennial women as leaders.

AUTHENTICITY AS NARRATIVE

Authenticity is a buzzword in management and leadership development (Avolio & Gardner, 2005; Goffee & Jones, 2005). Many organizations encourage individuals to be themselves at work and to completely merge their public and private identities. This contrasts sharply with the view that traditionally to be a professional would mean to put on a certain personality for work that masks one's real personality. I would first like to highlight some understandings of authenticity and would like to indicate how they are important not only for leadership development but also for Millennial women.

In order to define authenticity, let's start by looking at the definition the philosopher Martin Heidegger has provided (Heidegger, 1962). In *Being and Time* Heidegger uses the term *'eigentlich'*, which goes back to the German word *eigen*, referring to one's own. *Eigentlich* and the noun *Eigentlichkeit* is commonly translated as authentic or authenticity. *Eigentlichkeit* is contrasted by Heidegger (1962) to *Uneigentlichkeit*, which means being inauthentic. For Heidegger authenticity is situated on a continuum between being authentic and inauthentic. This means that one is more or less authentic. Heidegger's definition of authenticity means being true to one's own values. Rather than talking about authentic and inauthentic Heidegger (1962) suggests that we should talk about 'less' and 'more' authentic to denote the relativity entailed in authenticity.

We often presume that we have one stable self that does not change very much. However, as much of the academic literature on identities and in fact much of this book attests, the self is in fact fluid, shifting and flexible (Erickson, 1995). By that I mean that we are not always the same person but instead our behaviour and feelings are highly dependent on given situations. Our opinions and wishes change. What we perceive as a stable self is in fact a fiction that we create ourselves. This fiction is very important to holding identities together and to perceiving ourselves as stable throughout time. However, it is evident that in many cases who we are is dependent on our environment and on our own feelings. If authenticity is seen on a continuum, then this does not presume per se a stable self, but rather a flexible self. What constitutes the self is in fact how we make sense of ourselves or in more academic terms, create meaning about ourselves. This meaning in relation to authenticity is constituted by being true to what we perceive to be our self-values.

These self-values that define authenticity largely relate to self-awareness (Sparrowe, 2005). This means that authenticity is something that lies inside rather than something that can be found in relation to other people. For leadership development, authenticity is often seen as the enduring qualities of a leader through time and space, which is described as the inner self. Most importantly, this also refers to values. Authentic leaders are said to have an internal compass that guides them. In management research authenticity is often seen as self-knowledge, which is acquired through introspection (Goffee & Jones, 2005). By looking into ourselves we can become aware of our own feelings and thoughts. This self-reflection is critically important for human beings in general and for leaders in particular, and many leadership programmes foster this self-reflection. This goes hand in hand with being open about ourselves and becoming aware of parts of our self that we often try to ignore. In many cases the feedback of others is useful in providing us with information on how they see us and how this relates to our own perceptions of ourselves. For many individuals this means starting to reflect on how we tell our own stories. These personal histories will create an image of ourselves for others and us about what type of person we are.

Those narratives of the self or the way we tell our own stories are vital for how others perceive us. This presumes that our experience is mediated by discourse (Sparrowe, 2005). What does this mean? Rather than having pure experience, our experience is filtered through our interpretation. This interpretation of ourselves relates to culture, norms and values. When academics talk about meaning making, we often mean how individuals make sense of and interpret their own experience. These interpretations are always based on who interprets this experience, which makes it highly subjective.

In order to be authentic, individuals often create a dynamic plot that patches their experience together. We create ourselves by putting together different experiences in a story line that portrays us to ourselves and others in a certain light. The self is constant through the narrative. These subjective stories of ourselves are what it means to be authentic or being self-aware.

If authenticity is being self-aware, awareness of others is often seen under the umbrella of responsibility and ethics. After recent corporate scandals, developing ethical leaders is of prime importance of many business schools (Ghoshal, 2005). Values and business ethics are now compulsory in many business schools in the hope that this can diminish the risk of corporate scandals and financial crises in the future. Responsible leadership is therefore high on the agenda. Responsible leadership has been described as akin to stakeholder management in the sense that individuals who might be affected by the leader have the right to be heard by the leader (Maak & Pless, 2006). This means that a leader who is aware of others must create inclusion by building relationships to stakeholders, listening to their needs and concerns, and integrating those needs in any decisions and actions. Responsible leadership is therefore based on inclusion, collaboration and co-operation. While authenticity is often seen as relating only to self-awareness, an awareness for others is central in order to build one's own life story.

AUTHENTIC LEADERSHIP DEVELOPMENT

Authentic leadership development is often equated with constructing a life story that is seen by followers as authentic (Shamir & Eilam, 2005). This life story is going to give followers the required information to make judgements on whether or not this leader is perceived as authentic. In order to develop a life story it is important that the leader has the required self-knowledge and is clear about his or her values and convictions. This is often talked about academically as a self-concept. This self-concept has to be in line both with one's values and one's actions. Leaders' life stories are self-narrative ways through which an individual identity is constructed by linking them to space and time. Authentic leaders are able to present their life narratives as symbolic events in which one event happens after the other but the events are bound together by an overarching storyline which provides an answer to the question 'who are you'. These narratives need to provide justification for why one is a leader as opposed to others who are not. This answers the question 'why you are a leader'.

Research has identified four major themes or 'proto-stories' that leaders regularly use: leadership development as a natural process, as struggle and hardship, as finding a cause and as a learning process (Shamir & Eilam, 2005). Leadership as a *natural process* follows the pattern that either individuals were born natural leader and this was either evident from an early age or those natural abilities became visible only later on. Leadership development *out of struggle* means that instead of being a natural process, people had a defining experience that transformed them into leaders. Those stories also often stress the routes not taken. Leadership development through *finding a cause* often means that the leader emerges as part of a movement, for instance for social justice. This is particularly prevalent for political leaders. The fourth type of leadership development relates to *learning from experience*. Learning experiences can for instance relate to learning from failure or mistakes, and from positive or negative role models. Followers fail to draw on these 'proto-stories' to narrate their identities.

Developing a self-concept is a gradual process (Shamir & Eilam, 2005). Leadership development traditionally happens through experiential learning and formal education (which we will discuss in the next two chapters). These traditional approaches might be less helpful in developing an authentic leadership approach because of the highly individual nature of this process. The main way through which potential leaders can develop their own narrative is through having extended times for contemplation. It requires reflexive thinking. Apart from providing time to reflect on oneself, it is also important that the capacity to incorporate new events into the own life narrative. A guided life-review process can help to not only make sense of major life changing events but also the more mundane events (often called 'positive jolts') which can often give a wonderful insight into how a person acts and behaves. By thinking about 'positive jolts' potential leaders can reflect on what this contributes to their self-narrative. It is also important that the process of self-reflection is followed by a phase where the narrative is test driven to gain feedback on it. While this guided reflection might help leaders to develop their narrative, it needs to be remembered that the narrative has to convince their followers.

In sum, authentic leadership development has to start from the individual who needs to develop a self-narrative that often follows one of the four plot lines (leadership development as a natural process, out of struggle and hardship, as finding a cause and as learning process). Developing authentic leaders is, however, a highly individual experience and standardizing it in the form of experiential learning and formal education is difficult. Instead, leadership development has to focus on encouraging the self-reflexivity of potential leaders on past and current big and small events, which then can lead to the development of a self-narrative that is perceived as authentic by others.

THE PUBLIC AND THE PRIVATE

Traditional organizations were structured on a strict divide between the public and the private, which reinforced the gender division of labour. The public/private divide is built on the gendered divisions of labour: in the classic work of Parsons and Bales the public sphere requires the characteristics of logic and objectivity for which men's instrumental traits were ideally suited; women with their expressive skills were seen as unsuited for outside work but well suited for domestic tasks and bringing up children (Parsons & Bales, 1956). This ideal of the male breadwinner and the female homemaker establishes gender relations. The public/private divide is one of the core mechanisms through which the gender segregation of the workplace is upheld. Not only does it assign different spheres of work to men and women but it also attaches different skills to each. Masculinity is then bound up with instrumentality, whereas femininity is seen as expressivity. The division into a public and private sphere is therefore not only an underlying element of organizations, but it also reinforces the gendered division of labour.

However the divide between the public and the private has come under scrutiny with the rise of social media. Social media encourages individuals to create an online persona of themselves. Facebook, for instance, when announcing that its timeline will become compulsory for all users said the following 'Last year we introduced timeline, a new kind of profile that lets you highlight the photos, posts and life events that help you tell your story' (Facebook, 2012). The language Facebook has chosen to describe timeline stresses the ability of individuals to 'tell their own story'. This ability to tell their own story is a direct appeal to individuals to create an authentic self that is true to their values by selecting pictures and stories that represent them best. In addition, this authenticity is not just self-awareness but an orchestrated image that the Facebook user wants to convey to others by making certain images invisible and others visible. This authentic self transcends the public and private spheres.

For many Millennials the need to be authentic seems to be directly related to messages conveyed by social media to be themselves.

Social media allows individuals not only to document their life and tell their own life story but also to broadcast themselves (as the tagline of YouTube states). This means that the individual is now in control of their image much like in the past celebrities would manage their image. It is therefore not surprising that reality TV features 'ordinary' people who often rise to be celebrities in their own right. On top of that celebrities are now much more accessible; not only do their paparazzi images appear in newspapers and on websites, but many celebrities are also taking to Twitter to bring their own stories across. Singers Lady Gaga, Justin Bieber and Katy Perry are among the top Tweeters based on the number of their followers (Twitaholic, 2012). This makes the boundaries between celebrities and ordinary people more permeable and feeds the fiction that everyone can be a star. The only thing they need to do is to 'collect' enough social media 'friends'. Leadership for this generation is therefore increasingly defined by how many people they are connected to.

We have seen earlier that authenticity is a value that Millennials prefer and also that psychological narcissism has increased with this generation (Twenge & Campbell, 2008). Telling one's own story online seems to appeal to the narcissism of this generation. Research has explored the link between having an inflated image of yourself and feeling unique and special (or in psychological terms 'narcissistic') and the use of social media (Bergman et al., 2011). Differences were not detected in the number of friends, the time spent on social networking sites, the frequency of status updates, posting pictures or checking on social networking friends in regard to those individuals who have a more inflated image of themselves to those who do not. The research did however find that the reasons for engaging in social networking sites were different: Millennials who were higher on the narcissism scale were more likely to collect friends, wanting their friends to know what they are up to and trying to project a positive image through their profile. In fact, those Millennials with an inflated image of themselves seemed to act pretty much like a celebrity concerned about a positive image and collected followers/friends who were interested in what they are doing.

For Millennials the blurring of the public/private distinction goes hand in hand with the need to be authentic in a changing workplace. Many organizations try to appeal to Millennials by stressing that in their organizations people can be true to themselves. This will indeed appeal to many men and women of this generation for whom finding authenticity through telling their own story through social media and linking it to work is bound up with the feeling that they have little impact on their external economic environment.

WOMEN AS AUTHENTIC LEADERS

Authenticity narratives can be central for leaders to be seen as being true to themselves. Women in the workplace often struggle with the fact that they feel inauthentic in the workplace because they cannot bring their entire personality to work. Women regularly complain that they have to leave parts of their identity behind to be perceived as professional workers. This partly means managing the boundaries between the public and the private but it also means displaying appropriate behaviour. With the ideal worker being more masculine than feminine this means that many women feel that they have to give up their femininity in order to display the masculinity required of the ideal worker. The masculinity of the ideal leader is often described as gravitas and women are said to develop this gravitas themselves.

Authentic leadership is often achieved by leaders endorsing and conveying values that are relevant for their followers (Eagly, 2005). Research has often shown that communities tend to be represented by leaders who are prototypical for their shared belief in how a good leaders looks and behaves. If the ideal leader is seen as more masculine than feminine by men and women it is men who are more likely to be seen as leaders. This highlights the fact that there is an incongruity between the masculine leadership role and the feminine gender role that women are required to perform to be perceived as leaders. We have seen this in relation to the ideal worker. Women performing a leadership role are therefore often at risk of being seen as inauthentic by their followers.

Much of the leadership development for women has therefore focused on assertiveness training for women and allowing them to be themselves. Such an approach might however be less effective in building leadership potential (Eagly, 2005). Instead, research has suggested that women should tone down their femininity without emulating a masculine style. If women just adopt masculine styles this is commonly perceived as inauthentic by their followers, but stressing femininity might mean that one is not seen as suitable for a leadership position. In addition, women who clone male leaders might also appear inauthentic to themselves (Fenwick, 1998). This means that women have to display leadership by being masculine but not too masculine and feminine but not too feminine. Developing narratives that display this oscillation between masculinity and femininity therefore have the greatest chance of being perceived as authentic by followers and women themselves.

FITTING THE MOULD

In our interviews the idea of authenticity and being yourself at work resonated very well with most interviewees. It was interesting to notice that many Millennials talked about the experience of becoming a robot, fitting a mould or wearing a mask at work. When discussing leadership development approaches earlier on, one of the key elements was to avoid a replacement identity whereby people are replaced by others who look, speak and act just like those who they replace. This phenomenon of hiring in one's own image or having an ideal type to be recruited not only counteracts the idea of an authentic self it is also seen as one of the main mechanisms through which women are excluded from positions that were previously held by men. The idea of wearing a mask, becoming a robot and fitting a mould resonates strongly with the ideal worker in an organization who stands in sharp contrast to those who differ in one way or another from the implicit norm. These mechanisms surrounding the ideal worker exclude those who are different. They will also lead to the feeling in employees that they cannot be themselves at work. With authenticity being even more important when individuals feel like they have limited control over the outcome of their position, allowing employees to be themselves will provide the tools for them to build a consistent narrative of themselves.

The dominance of metaphors such as becoming a robot, fitting a mould or wearing a mask at work becomes visible in many stories that we heard from Millennials. Christine, for instance, said that that she would immediately join a company that would allow herself to be herself in the workplace but that she thought that this was highly unrealistic. She was definitely of the opinion that she had to fit a mould in her current job and that this is a fairly general feature of normal working life. Christine thereby confirms the importance of being herself at work but at the same time claims that very few workplaces really would allow you to be yourself. This indicates very clearly that many Millennials feel that they cannot unfold their entire personality in the context of work.

While Christine feels very much put into a certain mould, this is echoed by Eddie, who feels that he cannot bring his full personality to work. Eddie for instance describes himself as very loud and obnoxious but knows that if he brings this side to the workplace he might frighten a lot of people. Such an outgoing personality would be too much for his organization and he has to modify his behaviour to ensure that he does not cause offence. Eddie had taken specific steps to modify his behaviour.

Byron in contrast felt that his graduate programme would not transform him into robot. Instead he is given certain encouragements regarding how to be but is not forced to give up his personality. This is interesting in that Byron did notice the organization wanting to encourage a certain behaviour in people but he still feels that he can adopt that behaviour without becoming a robot. Becoming a robot would require too much energy for Byron. What Byron talks about is that there is a mutual shaping between the self and work which takes place which was expressed more explicitly by others such as Florence. She talked eloquently about how your job will rub off on your identity and how your identity will influence the type of job you chose. This mutual interplay is something that Millennials experience at work because this is for them one of the first chances to modify their identity in line with the requirements of work. While they were brought up being encouraged to be themselves, the workplace for many Millennials is one of the first exposures they get to an environment where they cannot be themselves but have to construct themselves based on organizational requirements.

One of the most striking examples of this mutual shaping between the professional and the private identities is provided by Imelda. Imelda is originally from the US and has decided to work in the UK to advance her career. She is slightly older than the standard graduate and worked in different companies before joining a graduate programme. She talks about how in her previous jobs she never felt that she had fully become part of the organization. She always retained part of herself or in other words an authenticity that existed outside work. She was most surprised that in her current work she felt that this separate identity was slowly breaking away. She started to identify fully with her organization and when describing her feelings she used the graphic example of having the company in her veins and arteries. This was surprising for her because before she had worked for an organization but did maintain some difference whereas now she literally feels as though she becomes one with the organization.

Through the interviews it became apparent that the imagery of becoming a robot, fitting the mould and wearing a mask at work became a metaphor Millennials used to describe the mutual shaping of work and self, which they either resisted or experienced. In most cases the Millennials felt in control of these shaping mechanisms. They felt in charge of either putting on another identity, putting on parts of it or rejecting it. Only in some cases, such as in Imelda's, did they feel little control over these activities and they were much more subtle. What is central here is that most Millennials felt in control of their authentic self and used it strategically in the workplace.

MANAGING YOUR IMAGE ONLINE

For many Millennials using social media has become a habit. They are used to updating their status regularly to let their followers or friends know what they are up to, and they document their lives by sharing pictures and stories. It is important to remember that not all Millennials will be glued to social media, but on average Millennials are more likely to engage with social media than other generations. The social media habit also means that the private life is increasingly public (even with the privacy settings on). This leads to various challenges in the workplace, where professionalism in the public sphere is expected. Some organizations are concerned that employees 'waste' too much time using social media and block it, while others try to embrace the new technologies for networking purposes. For Millennials, however, social media can turn into a real problem if the private and the public sphere converge too much. The example of Anton at the beginning of the chapter illustrates this. However, in many cases Millennials have developed a complex relationship to social media that is akin to managing one's identity online.

We can for instance look at Maya, who described herself as a 'Facebook addict'. She has over 750 friends on Facebook and she talks about how great the platform is for sharing information. Maya boasts about her large number of Facebook friends and it becomes evident in the interview that she collects those 'friends' and derives satisfaction from the fact that she has lots of friends. It seems to be the quantity of friends rather than the quality of friendships that matters here. At the same time, she also talked about privacy concerns. For instance, she would not connect with work colleagues as 'friends' on Facebook and she would not connect with her manager there. She asserted that this is not because she has anything to hide but rather because she likes to keep separate her work and private life. She goes on to talk about why she prefers to separate her work and private lives: she would find it highly unprofessional if a Facebook friend of hers puts pictures of her on a night out online which a work colleague might then see. For her this behaviour belongs to her private world and not in the workplace. She thereby draws a clear distinction between the public and the private identity she wishes to construct.

Another person to voice some reservations in regards to Facebook is Leela. Leela talked in the interview about how companies today are using Facebook in the recruitment process to find out as much as possible about a person. She thinks that this use of Facebook is wrong and it affects her online behaviour: Leela is very careful what she puts on her Facebook account. She does not want to miss out on a job or a promotion because she is not seen as the right type of person due to her Facebook profile. What is evident in Leela's account is the fact she is very aware of how her Facebook presence might impact her work life. At the same time she uses Facebook to share pictures and information with some other company graduates. She recounts how she has discussed with her network of graduates that they have to be careful what they say about their work and also their views. What Leela is aware of is the brand impact that this behaviour can have. Leela is not only a private individual but also an employee and even a casual remark that she supports a certain political party can be interpreted that the company she works for supports this party. In addition to revealing parts of her private life in the work context that might let her appear as unsuitable for a job or promotion, she is aware of the fact that she is also a spokesperson for the company and everything she posts online can be seen as the official opinion of this organization. She thereby is aware of the fact that she can affect the reputation of the organization, which in the long run might have repercussions for her career.

These are the reasons why some Millennials are not only very careful with their privacy settings, they are also thinking of withdrawing from Facebook and other social media altogether. Christine is a prime example of this. Like Maya she described herself as a bit of a Facebook addict. She talks about her joy of reconnecting with many friends from school with whom she had lost touch. For Christine this has to do with showing off as well – she can show everyone where she got to and how successful she now is. One is therefore in charge of telling one's story in such a way that it impresses others. Facebook and social media in general thereby become a way for engaging in impression management. Yet Christine has recently been considering deleting her online profile. The reasons for this are very similar to those that Maya and Leela mentioned. If people swear on her online profile or put up an image of her drinking, then this will impact negatively on her if her colleagues or managers see it. Christine is aware of the fact that not only can her current employer see that, also potential employers in the future can see those comments and images that might appear inappropriate.

In general, what we observed in the interviews is the fact that many Millennials were acutely aware of the dangers of social media for their professional identity. Millennials realized that social media is not private and that their current and future employers will check their profiles out. This means that they have to manage their own identity very much like a brand is managed. They have to ensure that they appear professional in the work context and that not too much of their private life spills over into their professional life. Moreover those Millennials realize that their expressions in the private sphere are not private anymore and become part of their professional self-image they need to construct. This means that many Millennials have to manage their social media profile with a view to their professional life. Being authentic is therefore no longer a question of bringing your entire self into the workplace, it is also a question of managing this private self in such a way that it appears professional.

LEADERSHIP DEVELOPMENT THAT BREAKS THE MOULD

After looking at some of the challenges and opportunities in relation to authenticity on- and offline, I would now like to take a closer look at what it means to develop authentic leaders. In the previous section we explored what types of people Millennials can identify with as role models, and one of the central constructs that emerged related to how authentic these individuals were. Managing one's social media persona to be professional was key here. In a sense Millennials already learn that authentic leadership does not mean being oneself at work but displaying a behaviour that is perceived by others as appropriate and professional.

When discussing authenticity it was however uncommon to make gender relevant in the process. This means that women did not voice their discomfort of being someone else at work more than men. In fact, both men and women expected to modify the way they behave at work to appear as professional. However, there were some gendered norms around this professionalism, which were mainly discussed when asked about gender in the workplace. Such norms for instance would relate to a different dress code, which we will discuss later on. For the moment it is important to state that when talking about being themselves at work the junior professionals we interviewed talked mainly about the pressures to manage their professional identities in relation to their private identities.

In many organizations leadership development is still a processes of cloning successful leaders. It is therefore important to take a look at examples that break the mould. One can reasonably expect that Millennials will resist the force to develop into leadership templates that are not in line with themselves. As a matter of fact many of the templates that are created in the workplace are modelled on narrow parameters, which support an ideal worker. This hinders not only women in being perceived as leaders but also many men who do not fit those leadership templates. This means for leadership development that a real effort is made to break away from templates that only allow certain people through who fit the template. Many Millennial women are implicitly ruled out of becoming leaders because it is expected that they will have children and this is all too often equated with no longer wanting a career. Millennial women will then either resign their ambitions because they cannot see themselves progress or they will attempt to fit in by complying to the masculine template to make a career. However, because they are perceived as women they will be seen as inauthentic in appearing too masculine. Both strategies will lead to Millennial women being disengaged from trying to be authentic leaders.

How can Millennial men and women be encouraged to be developed into authentic leaders? First, this involves management of the public and private spheres. Millennials are aware of the pressures to appear professional but, they are not aware of the fact that through carefully crafting stories from their private life into their professional life they can bolster their authenticity. Authenticity is then not just being oneself but rather creating a persona for oneself that others can see as a leader. Millennials thus need to learn to tell their stories in such a way that their private life enhances their professional life, which will mean closely monitoring and selecting which stories one tells. The four 'proto-stories' that leaders regularly use can be helpful in this. They included leadership development as a natural process, out of struggle and hardship, as finding a cause and as a learning process (Shamir & Eilam, 2005). We have seen that Millennials react positively to many of those proto stories in their own identification with role models such as the leadership development out of struggle, which was seen as one of the core characteristics of the self-made CEO/founder personality. Millennials need to start telling their life stories in such ways that they are perceived as leaders. This involves a careful management of how the private sphere moves into the public sphere. This requires feedback from others on how authentic the leadership narratives of individuals are.

Second, developing authentic leadership narratives for women will mean that they have to navigate the public/private and masculine/feminine boundaries. Millennial women should be open about their ambitions instead of waiting to be noticed. However, if women come across as too ambitious this will be perceived as too masculine and they are therefore going to be evaluated negatively by others as they violate the feminine gender role. Research on stereotypes has shown that if a stereotype is flagged up, it is easier to address it and the stereotypes are more likely to fall away. In regards to perceiving women as authentic leaders it would therefore help if women's leadership narratives include references to them being women and carefully include elements that are going to be seen as masculine and that are going to be seen as feminine. Millennial women need to craft carefully the stories that they will tell in the next promotion round. They are going to be highly individual, which is why I refrain from offering a template that can be emulated. These authentic leadership narratives will stem from Millennial women's own experience and are going to be told in such a way that they not only flag up gender but also play with masculinity and femininity to be perceived as authentic leaders. It is also important to encourage men to include feminine elements in their leadership narratives. This will then indicate that the ideal leader needs masculine as well as feminine elements. Men including elements of femininity in their narratives will widen the template in the long run and might lead to the fact that they feel more authentic, too.

SIGNATURE PRACTICE: ENVISIONING BEING A LEADER

Although many organizations claim to develop authentic leaders, there are few organizations that would help Millennial women to hone their authentic leadership skills. In order to become authentic leaders, it is important that Millennials develop identities that reflect their own self but that also resonate with others. We also know that women are often not perceived as authentic leaders because the leadership template is masculine and women do not fit within it. In order to provide Millennial women with individualized advise on how to progress their career, PwC Germany has developed a counselling programme where senior partners within PwC provide advice and feedback to Millennial women. The programme is unusual because it jumps various hierarchies and exposes fairly junior women to senior leaders in the organization. Similar to reciprocal mentoring discussed in the previous chapter, the idea behind this matching was the fact that junior women can learn from senior partners but also that senior partners can learn about what it means to be a junior woman in the organization. In order to reflect the hierarchical difference, the programme is called Up!Talk. Women who participate in the internal leadership development programme at PwC called the Young Excellence programme were selected to participate in Up!Talk. Whereas the Young Excellence programme provides formal and informal learning opportunities in a mixed-gender environment, the Up!Talk is able to offer a gender-specific element of receiving feedback for junior women. These women have been with PwC for three to four years and are in their mid- to late 20s.

While this would be called mentoring relationship in many places, PwC Germany selected the term 'counselling' to describe the relationship and to differentiate the programme from the mentor assigned to individuals as part of internal performance evaluation processes. The participants are called counselees and counsellors. The overall length of the programme is ten–12 months and follows the structure of first, a kick-off event with the counselees; second, a briefing of the counsellors; third, the counselees and counsellors are matched ensuring that participants work in different business units; and fourth, the matched pairs will meet at least four times face-to-face over the designated period.

The programme started in 2008 and is now facilitating the fifth cohort. To date, 58 Millennial women have participated in the programme. Of the 29 counsellors 17 of the councillors were men and 29 were women. The resonance of counselees on the programme is very positive: they talk about how they develop a vision for their future and how they are able to see that careers are not linear but are characterized by failures and false starts. These honest opinions are very different from the polished image that many partners would present about their career when talking in a formal setting. Millennial women also learn to receive feedback and act upon in. They also learn how difficult it is to give feedback to more senior people. In addition, the counsellors commented on their own learning and better understanding of Millennial women and how they have to modify their own management style to engage this group. Such honest feedback will help Millennial women to develop a vision of how their leadership identities might look and how they might be perceived as authentic by others.

Third, for Millennial women it is going to be of central importance to learn to find strategies for telling their own stories that reflect their strengths. While learning from mistakes and difficulties is important for leadership development, it is important to narrate these challenges in such a way that they are not self-defeating. It is important that men as well as women acknowledge challenges in their career stories, but they should be framed in such a way that they are turned into positive examples rather than being saturated with self-doubt. Given the construction of femininity in society, doubting oneself is a feminine trait that many women use to appear feminine. However, for potential leaders this self-doubt needs to be transformed into narratives of strength in which one turned a situation around rather than be defeated.

SIGNATURE PRACTICE: VIRTUALLY CRAFTING AUTHENTICITY NARRATIVES

Thomson Reuters, the business information provider, has noticed that developing authentic leadership stories is a central element of preparing women for senior leadership positions. As a global corporation Thomson Reuters operates in over 100 countries. Thomson Reuters was looking for a development solution for emerging female leaders based in different locations that would be scalable and cost efficient. This sparked the idea to pilot a virtual Women in Leadership programme with a focus on allowing women to develop authentic leadership narratives.

The virtual Women in Leadership programme is delivered via six online video meetings. The meetings focus on different topic areas designed to encourage reflection on developing an authentic leadership narrative. The first meeting features a female leader sharing her own leadership and career story. The remaining meetings focus on topics like exploring personal strengths, thinking through relationships to power, and developing a new approach to networking. All participants have to join the meeting during the allocated 1.5-hour time slot. After the meeting, they receive a recording of the session and are asked to complete some 'homework' to enhance their leadership development. Rather than offering a two-day intensive program, having six virtual meetings allows participants more time to absorb and integrate the learnt material. It also helps to build lasting networks with women from different countries and from different parts of the organization.

The pilot program was limited to eight participants. They were high performers and emerging female leaders but did not have to have been marked as high potential in their internal performance evaluations. Women in particular who were at a career transition or had recently started a new managerial role were asked to join because it was felt that the programme would have the most impact at this stage. Thomson Reuters also ensured that the women came from different functional areas and different locations in the world. In the first round of the programme the participants came from Thailand, China, Japan, India, Dubai, Switzerland, France and the UK.

The pilot programme was so successful that Thomson Reuters decided to expand the programme to 12 participants and to offer it to a greater number of women across the world. The feedback from participants of the pilot programme indicated that they had significantly advanced their self-awareness. The virtual Women in Leadership programme is not only an example of integrating authenticity narratives in leadership development for women but also shows that this can be delivered through virtual means on a global level.

Fourth, organizations can offer Millennials some structured guidance on how to develop their authentic leadership narratives and can raise awareness of bias. Leadership and talent development programmes can focus on developing and experimenting with authentic leadership narratives. This would allow aspiring Millennial leaders to reflect upon and receive feedback on their unique stories. When we selected interviewees for the study we wanted to allow Millennials to tell their own stories in their own words. The feedback that we received from Millennials was that they loved to have the time to reflect on themselves and work out their own identities. This indicates that Millennials enjoy talking about themselves. In addition, organizations include enough bias consciousness training to ensure that those who might not fit the leadership template at first sight are not excluded. Bias awareness training should ideally open the mind of employees to allow different narratives of individuals to count as authentic. We will discuss this in greater detail when we discuss the organizational cultures that will allow Millennial women to rise as leaders.

CONCLUSION

In this chapter we looked at authenticity and what it means for developing Millennial men and women into leaders. We defined authenticity as self-awareness that needs to be recognized by others so that they may perceive the leader as authentic. We have shown that Millennials prefer to bring their whole self to work and to be authentic. This is aided by social media, which encourages people to tell their own stories. However, Millennials also find that only some narratives are acceptable in organizations. It is therefore important for Millennials to develop self-narratives that reflect their experiences in the public and private spheres but to present them in such a way that others perceive them as authentic leaders. Receiving feedback and being able to act upon it is central. Given the fact that women are often perceived as inauthentic leaders due to the double bind, it seems important that Millennial women learn to include both masculine and feminine elements in their narratives in order to count as women and as leaders. In fact, including feminine elements in their narratives might also be a great way for Millennial men to develop as authentic leaders. Organizations should allow Millennials the space to develop and play with their self-narratives. They should also ensure that organizational members perceive a wide array of leaders as authentic by offering bias awareness training. After exploring self-knowledge through role models and authenticity, the next areas to explore are the processes of acquiring knowledge through experiential learning and formal education.

7

EXPERIENTIAL LEARNING — EVOLVING THROUGH FEEDBACK AND COACHING

INTRODUCTION

Following in her father's footsteps, Nicole decided to be a lawyer. After finishing law school, her father entered a medium-sized law practice in Australia, became partner of this law firm nine years after joining and to this day continues to work there. After finishing law school Nicole also joined a law firm, but she realized quickly that the pace of work there was fast. As the business model of law practices is based on billable hours, Nicole found that clients tried to squeeze out as much as they could. This often meant that Nicole had to work long hours. After a few years, Nicole decided that this lifestyle was not for her. She became a legal council with one of her clients whom she had advised before. While the pace of work was more manageable she decided that it was not only the workload that she struggled with but also the content of the job. She just did not want to be a lawyer anymore. After seven years as a lawyer she decided to follow her passion for aromatherapy and trained as an aromatherapist. To make ends meet, she started to work for a charity as their 'people' person. She really appreciated having a clocking in/out system. This limited her working time and she no longer works long hours. She is already thinking about her next career move, which will involve setting up her own company selling aromatherapy products. She hopes to open her own business within the next year, which is exactly nine years after she graduated from law school.

The careers of Nicole and her father evolved very differently in spite of a similar start. Her father worked for the same company in the same job for more than three decades. Nine years after graduation, Nicole will be in her fourth job and some would even say career, while her father was still in the same career and had just made partner. This illustrates that careers and life trajectories have changed and become more boundaryless. Boundaryless careers move between different employers, move laterally rather than hierarchically and require the ability to market one's own skills (Arthur & Rousseau, 1996). While the transition from a law practice to an in-house legal team was using Nicole's legal training and a similar range of skills, her move into aromatherapy, her role at the charity and her entrepreneurial ambitions require different skillsets. Nicole has to reinvent herself and update her skills. Reinvention requires constant learning.

For the Millennial generation learning is going to be more important than for any other generation. The half-life of knowledge describes the time it takes from gaining knowledge until when it is obsolete. The knowledge half-life is rapidly diminishing, requiring the individual to update their knowledge constantly. Learning is going to be one of the central axes around which leadership development for Millennials is going to take place. Developing Millennials and allowing them to learn will keep them engaged, which in turn will ensure that they stay longer with an employer, making the investment in them worthwhile. Acquiring knowledge is so important that I devote two chapters to this. The first of these chapters will look at experiential learning.

REINVENTING SKILLS AND CAREERS

It is often argued that careers are no longer stable, fixed and linear. Instead they are now often described as boundaryless (Arthur, 1994). Boundaryless means a career that is beyond one single organization. This might be sequentially or also in parallel. The purest form of the boundaryless career can be found, for instance, in graphic designers, who work for various clients at the same time. However, the boundaryless career also encompasses a much wider understanding by assuming that people will have different careers throughout their lifetime. For boundaryless careers the constant updating of skills is vitally important. This has been called self-programmable labour, denoting the ability to reskill constantly (Castells, 1996). If the individual stagnates and does not update his or her skills, this person will lose his or her employability. This is called employability security (Kanter, 1995). Rather than having employment security, having employability security means that one remains employable with different organizations.

A very good example of the requirement to learn and constantly stay up-to-date can be found in technology work. Technology has evolved quickly, meaning that people working in this area need to update their skills constantly. Research has, for instance, explored the emergence of web-design skills (Kotamraju, 2002). This research shows how early web designers tried to find a position between art and technology and how keeping up with the latest developments in the field was not only a required but also a necessary condition. It is shown how this process of skill evolvement is swift, indicating that the half-life of knowledge is decreasing. This constant re-skilling became the cornerstone of being able to sell one's own work. Skills become responsive to changes in technology and knowledge, and this process seems to be faster today than it was in earlier times. However, only those who are able to reinvent themselves are going to be able to secure their employability.

Experiential learning is important to maintaining employability. Experiential learning means learning from experience and through practice (Kolb & Kolb, 2005). Kolb (1984) argued that four inter-related processes are used to transform experience into learning: concrete experience (having an experience), reflective observation (reflecting on this experience), abstract conceptualization (learning from experience) and active experimentation (playing with what one has learnt). It is evident from this model that experiential learning means learning through experience by using reflection and abstraction. Experiential learning in organizations can take various forms, and I would particularly like to focus on how others can support this experiential learning, in relation to coaching and feedback.

Coaching and feedback mechanisms were the types of learning most regularly talked about by the Millennials. In this chapter I am going to work with Millennials' own interpretation of coaching and feedback rather than offer an academic interpretation of what feedback and coaching is. In research this would be called an emic understanding, which uses terms that people themselves use to make sense of their situation, rather than an etic understanding, which refers to the terms the researcher is imposing on the subject matter (Harris, 1976).

The activity that the interviewees described when discussing their ideal manager was one of a coach or mentor, and the behaviour that the coach or mentor should engage in was feedback. Feedback was a highly desired commodity for Millennials. They wanted immediate, constructive and constant feedback. The reason they were so keen on feedback related to the fact that they wanted to learn. They wanted to be better at what they are doing. They wanted to develop their skills. The need for feedback and coaching marks a departure from the ideal worker model, which assumes that the ideal worker is self-reliant and does not need external affirmation apart from slowly climbing the organizational ladder. Many managers of the

Millennials we interviewed seemed annoyed with that they had this constant need for feedback, which is why many see Millennials as demanding.

Let's take a closer look at the type of feedback Millennials want. Feedback is normally oriented backwards – it refers to past performance. However, in this context the feedback that Millennials wanted was future-oriented because it should improve performance. In educational research this has been called 'feeding forward' (Duncan, 2007). 'Feeding forward' (by the way an etic term), means feedback that is used to influence and improve future performance. Traditionally it is used in classroom teaching environments where feedback often comes too late, such as at the end of the term when an essay has been written and the teacher provides feedback on it. This will not help students improve. Feeding forward, in contrast, means in-sessional feedback that will influence performance in the final essay or exam. We will look at classroom learning in the contact of leadership development in the next chapter, but I would like to use the term 'feeding forward' to characterize the behaviour that Millennials engage in: they seek feedback to improve their future performance.

While feedback has been associated with improving one's performance, receiving feedback also contains potential threats to the ego and the self-image (Miller & Karakowsky, 2005). This means that it relates to self-confidence. To make most of feedback we need to be able to receive and to act upon it. As the average Millennial has high confidence and high self-esteem, Millennials should be able to deal with feedback in a constructive way. In fact positive feedback will feed their self-esteem. Feedback is also a way for Millennials to deal with ambiguity. We have discussed in regard to cross-temporal meta-analyses that Millennials are more likely to be anxious and depressed, which is particularly expressed in relation to ambiguous situations. In other words, not knowing if they are fulfilling expectations when expectations are not perfectly defined will fill Millennials with anxiety. The tendency to high anxiety might inhibit their ability to receive negative feedback.

However, we have also seen that Millennial women are likely to be more critical towards their own performance (Allmendinger, 2009). Successful women have often suffered from the so-called imposter phenomenon (Clance & Imes, 1978). This describes the inability of people to internalize their achievements. While there is a range of evidence that they are good at what they are doing, those women believe themselves to be frauds. The imposter phenomenon describes feelings of insecurity and self-doubt that 'someone is going to find me out and realise I don't really know what I'm doing'. Although research has not substantiated the fact that professional women are more likely to suffer from the imposter phenomenon than professional men (Fried-Buchalter, 1997), research on Millennial women (Allmendinger, 2009) suggests that Millennial women are more doubtful about their own performance than Millennial men. In the past, it has been argued that receiving feedback is beneficial for women because it helps them gain confidence (the same is true for men) (McCarty, 1986). While feedback might help mitigate the fact that women feel more nervous about their own performance, it might equally increase their self-doubt and the feeling that they are not good enough.

LEARNING THROUGH FEEDBACK

In our interviews feedback was something that the interviewees addressed to a great extent. Generally they felt that they did not get enough of it. This craving for feedback became particularly visible when the interviewees reflected on the behaviour of their ideal manager. We asked about ideal managers to get a better idea of how Millennials want to be managed and in particular what they are happy with and what can be improved. It was surprising to note how much feedback featured in the accounts.

A great example is Lyndon. Lyndon graduated recently from a top British university with a degree in sociology. For him an ideal manager provides feedback and a clear direction. The ideal manager, generally a 'he' in the accounts, also provides scope to grow. What was also important is the fact that the ideal manager would see Lyndon on an equal level, which mainly means listening to his input. Lyndon also addressed how he wanted responsibility to feel that he achieved an important part of the project while at the same time having easy access to the ideal manager who would provide advice. What Lyndon basically wants is someone who will help him to develop his ability. He wants someone who will help him grow. Feedback is essential because this can be used to enhance his performance.

However, the most vivid expression of how feedback features in the development of Millennials comes from Stefan. This account also gives us a clue as to the role technology plays in his craving for feedback. When asked how his ideal manager is supposed to be, he suggested that the ideal manager should be like a team leader in the World of Warcraft. For the benefit of those readers unfamiliar with the World of Warcraft, let me briefly explain what this is. The World of Warcraft is what is known as a massively multiplayer online role-playing game (MMORPG). Those are online worlds like Second Life where an avatar can be created who explores the virtual worlds (Childress & Braswell, 2006). The World of Warcraft, often called WoW, is another example of such an online world. Players are asked to buy a subscription to have access to the game. Each player gets an avatar who can learn new skills ranging from professional qualifications to hobbies. The avatar is usually given a mission to accomplish which is called a quest. Often these quests involve fighting. If a quest has been completed the player is rewarded with a prize such as virtual money or additional experience. Players can play individually or form groups or teams. While one might assume that such games of questing and fighting appeal more to adolescent men, market research counted 675,713 unique male players and 428,621 unique female players in the age group 25–54 in the US (Nielsen, 2009). Even though the reliability of virtual gender is always questionable, it is interesting to note that the gender differences are not as great as one would assume.

The fact that Stefan, a married German citizen working in London, used World of Warcraft to describe his ideal manager is fascinating and an ideal way to explore the nature of feedback that Millennials want. First, Stefan wants to know from me if I know what the World of Warcraft is. One of the key skills for academic interviews is always to allow research participants to explain everything to you. In fact, this is often called being an 'incompetent learner', which means that even though one might know about something one always denies it to encourage the participant to explain it again in his or her own words (Lofland & Lofland, 1984). This helps researchers develop emic understanding (which sometimes comes to haunt you in everyday conversations; I habitually deny knowing about something). I, of course, denied that I knew about the World of Warcraft and Stefan explained to me that it is an online computer game and that a recent study shows that one can actually learn leadership skills and transfer them from a virtual environment into reality. IBM and Seriosity have indeed produced a report that argues that leadership skills gained in virtual worlds can be useful in the real world (IBM & Seriosity, 2007; Reeves & Malone, 2007). Such a study is used here to argue that playing an online game can develop one's abilities in real life, and so establish credibility for online gaming.

After establishing the credibility of his use of the World of Warcraft for leadership development, through reference to research, Stefan went on to specify what it is that he actually learns through the World of Warcraft. He singled out immediate feedback, which is critical for his performance. He said that his perfect leader gives feedback immediately, be it positive or negative, and then rewards individuals accordingly, also immediately. Stefan continued to specify what that means in his work context. He wanted his manager to tell him what was good and what was wrong either on the day or after a project is complete. The ideal manager should also encourage him to improve those elements that were not good. Stefan would experience this as motivating and fair. However, Stefan dislikes that in his current job in a consultancy he only gets feedback on his performance every six months (and his reward only within a year's time). That is too long for him. He wants feedback and rewards that are much closer to his actual performance. Six months later the feedback that he might get will be less useful to improving his performance because he might not even remember the project well.

Stefan was particularly focused on reward. This was not often expressed that clearly but was often implied. This should not come as a surprise to us given that the research on Millennials has indicated a strong focus on rewards, particularly financial ones (Twenge, 2010). However, Stefan's example tells us much more about the nature of feedback and its origin. Most Millennials we spoke to talked about the constant, immediate and constructive feedback they wanted. In fact, the type of feedback that many Millennials wanted strongly resembles the interactions they have on social media. With Facebook and Twitter, for instance, a live stream updates your friends and followers with news about you. People normally react quickly to these messages, and if a tweet or post has not attracted much attention shortly after it is posted, it is unlikely to attract more later. In other words, few people would post a comment on your post or re-tweet it six months after the event. Yet that is how much of the feedback is structured in organizations. It lags behind the event by quite some time, and unlike with social media you might not even have documented this specific task that you receive feedback for. In other words, the nature of the feedback that Millennials want resembles the type of interaction they experience using social media.

While constant, constructive and immediate feedback was welcomed by Millennials, they were also clear on what they did not want from a manager: micromanagement. Dan, for instance, prefers his managers to tell him what the problem is and how long he has to solve it. He prefers a manager to offer support when it is needed, but otherwise to let him get on with it. He dislikes anything that smacks of micromanagement. Ian followed a similar approach, saying that micromanagers make him uncomfortable but he welcomes having checkpoints with his manager. Imelda also voiced that she flourishes under managers who give her a remit, tell her what the end goal is and allow her to get there on her own. Christine was even more outspoken about micromanagers, saying that she hates them. She wants to be left alone once she has been given clear expectations.

While Millennials craved feedback, they also did not want to be micromanaged. One might regard this as somehow contradictory, because micromanagers provide constant and immediate feedback. However, the activity itself seems very different. A micromanager checks up on the person he or she is managing. This implies a lack of trust in the ability of those one is managing. It is not about developing the individual but rather ensuring the project is delivered. However Millennials with their maybe slightly inflated self-confidence want to be trusted. They believe that they can deliver the parts entrusted to them if briefed properly. At the same time, they want to learn from what they did wrong and what they did well to improve their performance. A micromanager does not have development at heart but control. This changes the interaction and explains why Millennials want lots of feedback as soon as possible: it develops them in a constructive way. Detesting micromanagers means detesting people who do not trust Millennials and constantly check on them without much interest in developing them.

It is here that we see how the behavioural patterns of Millennials in the workplace have changed due to their exposure to social media. Although some Millennials might be highly sceptical about social media and see the potential risks, at the same time it appears that these types of interaction structure the nature of feedback they want. Rather than technology being just a tool that Millennials engage in, we see that it affects the expectations they have in the workplace. The example of the World of Warcraft is a metaphor for how virtual experiences lead to the real life expectations that many employers face. The wide-reaching consensus that Millennials want feedback on their performance as soon as possible is likely to be meditated by their experiences with social media, but it also points to the wider need to develop themselves. They want feedback that develops them, which is why they dislike micromanagers who are not interested in developing their employees. This becomes particularly clear when we look in the next section at the regularly voiced wish for coaches and mentors.

COACHES TO GUIDE DEVELOPMENT

Coaching and mentoring came up with persistent regularity when the ideal manager was discussed. This already started to shine through in the previous section, in which feedback was often seamlessly linked to coaching. Coaching, like feedback, was strongly linked to self-development. Self-development is indeed the underlying aim that many Millennials have to ensure they keep learning. It also circles back to authenticity because through coaching Millennials often want to receive feedback on how authentic they appear.

Harry bemoaned the fact that he felt that in the organization there was no one who would take responsibility for seeing him grow. He felt very much left alone when it comes to training and development and his career progress. While he acknowledges that there is a careers counsellor who should help him plan his career, he voiced the frustration that this person would not provide the 'correct' type of advice. He wanted more business-centred advice whereby he could learn from current projects. He also wanted someone with whom he could work out his development priorities: which projects should he work on to develop into a better professional? Harry felt that he was not being given individual and tailored advice. In his words, he wanted to be mentored. This was echoed in many accounts and often meant that the Millennials we interviewed just wanted to spend time with their manager. Harry talked about how his manager in an ideal world would spend two to three hours every week with him going through what was good and what could be improved, and this detailed analysis of work would provide him with the type of feedback he needs to develop his learning.

A similar type of comment was provided by Charlotta, who came from Finland to study in the UK. She was a very strong student at university and achieved top academic results. However, for her it was also important to find the right type of job. After spending a year as an exchange student in China, she had various offers from different companies but was not sure which one to take. The careers service in her university focused on providing advice on different careers and on how to survive assessment centres. However, Charlotta felt that the traditional career service at her university would not necessarily help her make the right choice for her career development. What she needed was some coaching whereby another person would talk her through the different options available to her and what the pros and cons would be. She needed somebody impartial who is not invested in any of those choices but is able to provide her with support to consider and evaluate her options. In other words, she needed someone to reflect with and who would guide her thinking.

Millennials are often keen to feel part of a group and to gain support from this group and particularly its manager. Again Stefan, who we met before when we explored the World of Warcraft, provides a great example for the type of bonding Millennials enjoy. Stefan talked about how he had just joined the team of a new manager who has the reputation of being 'the best' in the company. Stefan likened joining his team to joining the 'mafia', which was a curious term to use. Stefan explained that his manager manages his team closely, which is facilitated by the fact that the team works on client sites and so develops strong bonds. The team constantly exceeds expectations. Stefan also stated that once you join the team you are unlikely to get out. This inability to leave the team is probably why Stefan chose to use the term 'mafia' to describe the team. Stefan continued to explain that the team, and particularly the manager take care of you. Stefan realizes that his manager is in a great position internally to support him. This applies on the one hand to the promotion processes, in which managers are regularly called up to speak for (or against) individuals, and means that building a strong relationship with your manager is important in allowing him or her to speak for you. This advocacy is akin to sponsoring. The orientation towards career progression speaks to the often-discussed impatience of Millennials to advance.

However, this wish to advance is bundled with the wish to learn more. And this is exactly where Stefan feels his mafia team is falling short: he describes his role in the team as boring. While he enjoys the friendly banter and community with his team colleagues, he is not learning as much as he wants to. He said that is unable to climb the 'ladder of knowledge' through the project. Stefan is aware of the fact that this project might get him promoted but he will not be a better consultant through it because he does not learn enough. He particularly wishes that his manager would provide him with more meaningful work that would allow him to broaden his skills spectrum. While his manager is strong internally and will be his sponsor, this is not enough for Stefan. He also wants to learn as much as possible and his manager is not taking his learning seriously enough.

Being coached to learn also came through in Rupali's comments. Rupali is originally from India, and after studying in the UK she was recruited into a graduate role there. Rupali is hungry for experience and she recognizes that working with her current organization is a huge opportunity. Rupali talked about how she wanted to be coached by her manager. She does not want to be micromanaged and wants to have as she said 'a bit of freedom' in doing her work. She wants to have responsibility and she wants to be challenged and stretched by her assignments. She recognizes that she does not have a lot of experience at this stage in her career and she therefore appreciates developmental feedback from her manager. Rather than just being told what to do, she wants to receive developmental feedback through open conversations with her ideal manager. An ideal manager should be a coach who wants to develop her through challenging assignments.

A similar sentiment was voiced by Byron. Interestingly, he talked about his ideal manager as paternalistic. Paternalistic refers to the traditional relationship between father and child, which is governed by rules and regulations of what not to do. I was intrigued that he used such an unusual way of describing an ideal manager because paternalism is often associated with restrictions and an *Unmündigkeit*. *Unmündigkeit* means directly translated from German being minor of age and the literal translation is being unable to speak. Legally in means not being able to enter contracts. It therefore implies immaturity and dependency.

How does it happen that Byron uses 'paternalistic' to describe his ideal manager? Byron wants a manager to develop him professionally but also privately. Byron realizes that sometimes it is necessary to be strict. The ideal manager should be interested in him and his development over the next five years. He does not want to be seen as yet another graduate but as an individual who can be developed to perform better at his job. While I first thought that paternalistic might not have been the word he is looking for, it seems to be exactly what he wants. He wants a strict father but a father who wants the best for his child. Byron thereby sees himself as in a dependant (*unmündig*) position and he wants to be developed as a person by someone who is like a strict father to him.

While the paternalistic manager was not an ideal widely looked up to, many Millennials talked about coaching and mentoring as mechanisms through which they can learn. Kim provides a wonderful example for this. She said that she wanted a coaching manager. She does not want her manager to fix a problem for her, but instead tell her what to do, so she knows how to solve the issue the next time it comes around. Eddie and Imelda provided similar examples of a manager who coaches and develops.

In all, the coaching manager was seen as the ideal form of manager. Coaching was so important for the Millennials because they wanted to be developed. As with feedback, having a coaching manager was seen as essential to developing at work. The Millennials wanted to develop to be better at their jobs. At work a manager almost turns into a parent who looks out for them, gives them interesting work and distributes criticism where it is due. Millennials want to be looked after and cared for. This might have different implications for mid-level and senior men and women. Reflecting the traditional gender distribution of parenting roles, it might be that Millennials expect more senior men to be more like a stern father figure whose approval is sought, whereas they might want to see more senior women as mother figures who are emotionally caring and nourishing.

LIVING WITH INSECURITY

In this chapter we have explored how Millennials talk about their ideal manager to find out what types of behaviours motivate them. What has become very apparent is the fact that feedback and coaching are centrally important for them. Feedback and coaching in fact fulfil similar functions: they provide ways through which the individual's performance can be improved. One could presume that this type of self development is yet another expression of their 'narcissism' (in psychological terms). However, in this case the need to improve their performance might run much deeper.

When asked about how their careers are going to be different from their parents' many Millennials talked about the fact that their parents stayed with a company for an extended period of time. Ian said that his parents' generation had jobs for life. He particularly notices that among his clients many have been with the same employers for 30 years or more. He also talks about one of his colleagues, who decided at 35 that he wanted to go to medical school. Ian thinks that in previous generations it would just not have been possible to change careers that 'late' in life. Ian is generally very conscious of the fact that change in general is now much more fast paced, which means that one has to keep learning new things. He is aware of the fact that the knowledge he has now will become obsolete. This means that one continually has to learn.

That becomes particularly clear in William's account. When he talked about his parents' generation he acknowledged that at this time people would just expect a job for life and were therefore loyal and committed to the organization. In his view one then expected to be looked after by the firm. This has changed completely. In fact, William talked about how his own father was made redundant, which he described as feeling 'a bit like a kick in the teeth'. His described his father as working long and hard for the organization and yet the company made him redundant. This has led him to the attitude that one has to look out for oneself and to plan for the worst. He is also of the opinion that one has to enjoy life and not live life based on delayed gratification. An example he quotes is how his parents' generation saved money in pension funds towards retirement yet he is aware that they can just disappear. For him this means that saving for the future makes little sense, because it can be wiped out at any moment.

What emerges from this account and was present in many others, too, is the fact that jobs for life are perceived by this generation as a thing of the past. They also show a fundamental distrust of the traditional system of delaying gratification and instead support an ideology of immediate enjoyment. In a world where certainties can disappear overnight, there is no more ensuring for security and the individual has to brace him or herself for the worst. A world full of insecurities emerges. Rather than seeing this as a depressing factor, Millennials seem to have incorporated insecurity as the *status quo* into their mindset. They accept that the world has changed and that this means that they need to live now, but also that they need to ensure that they retain their employability through learning.

The reason why this generation might be more 'narcissistic' in psychological terms may be that they have learnt that changes in the world of work mean that they have to look out for themselves and have to ensure that they stay on top of their game. This means getting as much feedback on their performance as possible and it means searching for people who can help them develop their skills. It means learning continually to ensure that they will find jobs elsewhere if need be.

It does not mean, however, that Millennials are disloyal. While Millennials are often characterized as job changers and as uncommitted, this is not necessarily the case. Following the logic previously outlined, Millennials are happy to stick with an employer as long as they are able to learn. This means feedback and coaching, but it also means challenging work and assignments. Christine, for instance, talked eloquently about how being stretched and being challenged was central to keeping her happy. It was also a way to learn new things. Harry specified that he likes the intellectual stimulation in his current job, which allows him to learn.

FEEDING FORWARD TO ENSURE EMPLOYABILITY

What does this mean for organizational practices? Let's start with feedback. While immediate, constant and constructive feedback would be ideal, for many organizations this is unrealistic because it would put too big a burden on often already overworked middle managers. However, while support from more senior people in the hierarchy would be perfect, in many cases Millennials are open and receptive to peer feedback. Peer networks that allow Millennials to share experience could for instance be set up on- and offline. Online training in the form of video games can add a dimension to feedback and learning (Yee, 2006) but traditional classrooms continue to be important places for learning (see next chapter). In addition, advice on performance can be shared by senior professionals through online networks, and many Millennials would profit from it. This is not necessarily the individual relationship that many Millennials crave, but it would give them additional sources of feedback and advice.

SIGNATURE PRACTICE: GROWING THROUGH COACHING AND FEEDBACK

Many organizations faced with the question of how to develop their junior female leaders contemplate whether to use single-sex or co-educational talent development programmes to change the make-up of the gender pipeline. In 2005, Baxter International's Asia Pacific region has, under the leadership of Gerald Lema, set the ambitious goal of achieving gender parity at management levels across the region. Baxter's Asia Pacific region encompasses Australia and New Zealand, China, Japan, South East Asia, India, and North Asia. This was not an easy goal for the healthcare company in this region. In 2004, only 25% of leaders were women. However, by 2009 the critical gender balance of 50% men and 50% women had been achieved. This was mainly due to an initiative called 'Building the Talent Edge'. This is a talent management initiative focused on creating a 50/50 gender balance in leadership positions across the region through recruitment and development strategies, paired with increased communication and accountability.

A key component of the initiative was the GROW programme, which is a one-year intensive programme for high potential managers that should help them enhance their leadership skills and capabilities. Alongside top performance, gender balance is a key criterion for selection, and across the regions roughly 50% men and 50% participate in the programme. Rather than offering a women-only programme, Baxter decided that gender and diversity and inclusion competence is something that all future leaders need to display. The GROW programme is delivered on a country level, with a dozen country-specific programmes currently in operation. Each year-long programme consists of 26 people and is delivered in the local language wherever possible. GROW includes 360-degree feedback, coaching and classroom learning. Coaching and feedback allows participants to reflect on their own performance and to modify their performance in the future. This is not only a critical component of leadership development, it is also an activity that is appreciated by Millennials for enhancing their learning.

Organizations might also try to shorten performance review cycles to ensure that Millennials get feedback on their performance more quickly. Although this will put an extra strain on resources, in some organizations it might be possible to tweak the performance evaluation cycles to help Millennials to achieve the critical feedback they want. Moreover, it is vitally important to explain to Millennials what type of feedback they are receiving and when. Often they might not recognize feedback as such and it often helps to point to the specific ways a manager and an organization distributes feedback.

It is crucial that the overall performance evaluation system includes a strong focus on developing and coaching others. In fact, leadership development should focus on strengthening the skills that good coaches have: listening carefully and showing potential future pathways to individuals. Having coaching managers who see the development of others as a crucial skill will be the model for the future. However, many performance evaluation systems rely on the individual or others to report on this behaviour. This entails the problem that the individual will of course focus on the positive, and many others who are invited to provide feedback will do likewise. Little evidence is given, however, of how these skills play in out action. Rather than relying on oral and written accounts, a novel approach for leadership development might, for instance, be to observe leaders in the workplace and to collect evidence for when they show a certain type of behaviour. Such leadership development tools would clearly only be available to the most senior members of organizations due to the fact that it is resource intensive. However, it might provide new insights into which behaviour a coaching manager in a specific organization shows.

Are there gendered patterns in regard to experiential learning? Our research did not uncover gendered patterns that would highlight that Millennial men and women want something different from their ideal managers. In contrast, it was surprising to see that there was a lot of overlap between the replies provided by men and women. Millennials seem confident enough to take on feedback to develop themselves. What is also intriguing is the fact that the eulogized ideal manager of Millennial men and women was one who shows nurturing qualities. However, this developmental feedback might take different forms when performed by male and female mid-level managers and leaders. Here the expectation of Millennials might be that more senior men are the stern father, whereas women are the emotionally supportive mother. This is a dramatic departure from how ideal managers were perceived in the past and one might say that this nurturing and caring can be stereotyped as more feminine. Helping others to evolve might be more of a feminine trait, but it is clear that, regardless of their gender, the managers and leaders of the future will have to display those skills in order to provide Millennials with the feedback they crave.

CONCLUSION

For Millennial women to develop as leaders, it is important that they leave their comfort zone and learn through experience. In this chapter we have looked at why it is so important for Millennials to learn. We did this exploring how Millennials describe their ideal manager. It became apparent first that Millennials appreciated constant, immediate and constructive feedback. We traced the type of feedback back to behaviour learnt through social media and online games. Second, we looked at the coaching manager who has the interest of the Millennial at heart when advising him or her. Here managers are seen as sounding boards that listen to what Millennials have to say and advise them on what would be best for their career development. Feedback, as well as the coaching manager, follows the same logic because both elements contribute to learning. Learning was perceived as central to the Millennials, as they recognized that jobs for life are no more and that one has to be able to reinvent oneself. This is only possible if one is at the top of one's game. Due to the change of taken for granted certainties into uncertainties Millennials are more likely to shun the idea of delayed gratification and might therefore decide to live in the here and now. Yet for many Millennials the ultimate reward seems to be fairly traditional hierarchical progression in the organization, which is taken as proof of one's good work. What has been interpreted as a lack of commitment in Millennials is rather the need to be motivated by learning through challenging assignments, feedback and advice on self-development. It thereby emerges that by engaging Millennials and giving them ample opportunities to learn through feedback and coaching, they are confident that they might be employable elsewhere, which seems to increase their happiness at work and the likelihood of them staying with the organization. While traditionally women have been presumed to suffer from low self-confidence and the imposter phenomenon, which might limit their abilities to incorporate feedback to improve their performance, this research shows that Millennial men and women do not differ in their wish for feedback. The ideal manager, however, is increasingly transformed into a nurturing parent who helps the Millennial to develop.

8

FORMAL EDUCATION — LEARNING AS A RITE OF PASSAGE

INTRODUCTION

Iara had made good progress since joining an investment bank in Brazil. However, after four years with the bank, she felt that she had reached a career plateau. A natural progression in her job would be for her to take the role of her manager, but her current manager was only a few years older than she was and it did not look like he would be going anywhere soon. Iara began to research other similar positions but within the bank very few options seemed available. It was at this time that she started to think about an MBA. She had completed her undergraduate degree in mathematics and felt that more exposure to business thinking, as well the self-developmental aspects of an MBA programme would suit her well. It might provide her with the necessary tools to advance in her bank, or any organization for that matter. She started to research MBA rankings and entry requirements. She thought that an MBA degree would only make sense if it came from one of the top schools. Otherwise she felt that the opportunity costs were too high. She did not only have to pay her student fees and her maintenance but would also miss out on her regular salary, which she had grown accustomed to. With her family's resources already stretched to the limit, she would have to take out a loan. She chose a small number of elite MBA programmes. These programmes were selective and not only wanted a high general management admission's test (GMAT) score but also an impressive professional and personal background. Iara was very happy to receive offers from two top MBA schools. After visiting both schools, she decided on her favourite and joined the next intake.

She generally loved the experience of doing an MBA and particularly the time she had available. After working full time for four years, she had forgotten how much time students have. She was able to think about her own ambitions and how she wanted to develop.

115

The in-class teaching provided her with stimulating thoughts. The material was challenging and on some days she felt like the dumbest person in class. On other days she thought that she was the smartest. She felt that the MBA was transforming her views, opinions and her sense of self. Her classmates were both friends and people from whom to learn a great deal, and she formed strong bonds with them. Almost all of her private life evolved in the business school. She loved participating in competitive sports and joined the female ruby team. There were many visits to the student bar with her classmates that often ended in heavy drinking.

While she enjoyed student life to the full, there was something in the air that meant that she sometimes did not feel very comfortable. She had not failed to notice that women only accounted for 26% of her cohort. Most of the activities were oriented towards men and she felt that her MBA degree was teaching her a lot about how men behave and how she too could become an honorary man. What she experienced was being in a gender minority. For the first time in her life, it dawned on her that if she wanted to pursue a life as a senior manager this would be the type of environment she would find herself in. While the experiences of developing into a leader were widely discussed and debated in business school, there was little room to discuss gender-related issues. Most of those reflections happened in Iara's own mind; only sometimes did small groups of women come together and touch on the gender issue. There was also a Women in Business Club, which was one of the few places where gender was openly discussed. However, both men and women in her cohort agreed that the Women in Business Club was another way of getting face time with recruiters rather than advancing any political interests on behalf of women.

Iara's experiences are not atypical. For many MBA students the MBA feels like a rite that they have to pass in preparing themselves to become senior managers and leaders in organizations. For many women the MBA experience also prepared them for the male-dominated environment that senior managers and leaders inhabit. In this chapter I will look at the MBA as an example for formal education for Millennials and particularly focus on the gendered elements contained in doing an MBA. The chapter will start by explaining the rite of passage and discussing some prior research on gender in business schools.

RITES OF PASSAGE

It is often claimed that it is vital for future leaders to hone their skills by studying for an MBA degree. The MBA has in fact become a rite of passage. The rite of passage is an anthropological concept developed by French anthropologist Arnold van Gennep (Van Gennep, 1960). This concept is used to describe changes in status, such as the status change from being a junior to being a more senior professional. Anthropological research has highlighted the rituals that are attached to transitional stages in one's life.

Van Gennep identifies three phases through which an individual progresses as he or she changes status: separation, transition (or *liminal phase*) and incorporation. In the separation phase individuals are first taken out of their normal processes and routines. They leave their old selves behind. In the second, liminal phase, the individual plays with a range of identities to see which ones fit. This helps them determine who they want to be. In this stage it is important to be separated from normal routines so as to allow alternative identities to emerge. The person also learns new skills by, for instance, completing difficult tasks. The person is prepared for increased responsibilities. Those who undergo the rite of passage tend to develop an intense camaraderie, called 'communitas' (Turner, 1969: 95). In communitas the distinctions of rank and status are homogenized and therefore ignored. In other words communitas is shaped by egalitarianism. The final stage is incorporation. In this phase the identity is stabilized and the individual rejoins society. The rejoining of society should be at a higher or more prestigious level.

It is not difficult to see how doing an MBA degree will follow a very similar pattern. First the individual leaves his or her job behind. Normal routines and responsibilities fade into the background. During an MBA different avenues of change are explored. New skills are developed and new knowledge is acquired. Finally the newly minted MBA re-enters the world of work in hopefully a higher position and with the right skills to be a future leader.

For leadership development the time spent doing the MBA is particularly interesting because it represents a liminal phase when different identities are 'tried on' and new skills are formed. Formal educational settings are a prime example for such liminal spaces because they afford the individual the time and space needed to grow. This environment is free from the pressures of work. One meets new people and previous identities are less important. An MBA degree offers one of the few chances in working life to start with a *tabula rasa* in regard to one's working identity. This new self is then positioned in the labour market ready to take more responsibilities. The rite of passage concept therefore allows us to understand some of the processes that are induced by formal education. I will draw mainly on MBA education because this formal education is still perceived as crucial to developing as a future leader in organizations.

GENDER AND MBAs

The concept of the rite of passage might suggest that during the liminal phase we can take on any identity we want. While this stage certainly encourages a playful approach to identity, we should not forget that traditional markers of identity, such as gender, class and 'race' influence the types of identities we can adopt. However, very often those markers of differences are ignored by MBA students themselves because acknowledging them would mean that potential selves are actually limited by those markers. In addition, it would mean introducing divisions into the otherwise carefully crafted 'communitas', which is built on the ignorance of difference. Exploring how experiences during an MBA programme are gendered is therefore a useful angle for exposing the fact that the withering away of markers of identity like gender that individualization proclaims is more complex in reality.

Individualization refers to a situation in which individuals are increasingly required to shape their own lives (Beck, Giddens & Lash, 1994). Rather than being born into a certain class, profession and gender, people now become aware that they can make choices about who they want to be. They do not expect any traditional markers of identity such as gender to influence their chances of success. This means that today many paths appear open and it is up to us to decide which paths we want to take. Millennials in particular have grown up with the belief that they can be whoever they want to be.

As I have argued earlier, the choice of who one wants to be is in reality much more restricted. It still depends on whether one is born into a developing or developed country and which skin tone one has. It also matters which social and human capital one is bestowed with, which is often a function of class. Gender is of course still important in a workplace which is horizontally and vertically segregated (Charles, 2003). This means that men and women are working in different areas of work, with women not choosing to work in science, engineering and technology, for example. In addition, there are few women at the top of organizational hierarchies. It is often argued that women just choose to opt out of climbing organizational ladders and studying science, engineering and technology. However, what appears to be a choice is largely the result of a gendered socialization that tells women that if they want to flaunt their femininity and count as women in society, they had better not study science, engineering and technology because these are things for men. Similarly, many women will be influenced by the fact that being a senior leader follows a masculine template and so their choice against becoming a senior leader is also a choice against the masculine template.

A similar issue can be observed among women entering MBA degrees. The top MBA schools regularly report a gender imbalance for MBA intake. The *Financial Times* assesses the top MBA schools every year using a range of criteria, of which gender composition of the student body is one (*Financial Times*, 2012). The top ten global MBA students have on average 34% women students (*Financial Times*, 2012). Given that gender composition is one of the criteria used in the ranking, the top ten business schools can be expected to be good performers on gender diversity, and many other schools have even slightly lower percentages of women. Whereas undergraduate business education is gender balanced, an MBA still seems to be a choice taken by more men than women.

The relative paucity of women on MBA programmes mirrors the roughly 30% of women in mid-level management positions. Viewed hierarchically it is an expression of vertical segregation, which leads to the question of why this vertical segregation re-establishes itself. There is ample literature on why women do not enter MBA programmes (for an overview, see for instance Sinclair, 1995). First, it is regularly claimed that women lack the mathematical skills needed for an MBA and therefore shy away from considering an MBA. Second, it is suggested that doing an MBA coincides with the time when women are considering starting a family. Given the considerable investment an MBA requires, it is argued that women cannot recoup this investment if they are planning to reduce their working hours to bring up their children. Third, and of major importance for this chapter, is the culture of MBA programmes. Courses are mainly delivered by male professors via case studies that focus on men and men's interests; the absence of women from such samples in research cited in the classroom is often ignored. Much learning on MBA programmes is done in teams in which women often find that their ideas, comments and contributions are ignored, overruled and dismissed. Competition and instrumentalism, which are often seen as expressions of traditional masculinity, predominate in the classroom. The culture outside the classroom is dominated by heavy drinking and extreme sports, which women might find less appealing. This suggests that the choice of women against an MBA is also structured by the masculine culture that many MBA programmes provide.

119

This is particularly problematic because the skillset of future leaders is said to require emotional and social competence (Fletcher, 2004). While traditional or heroic leadership relied on instrumentality, this post-heroic leadership requires emotional and social competence. The latter are most commonly associated with femininity. Thinking back to how Millennials want to be managed, it was apparent that they want to be coached and developed. These activities require leaders and managers to have emotional and social competence. Yet these competences do not seem to be developed in an environment which values masculinity through instrumentality and competition. One could therefore state that the masculine culture of MBA education is not only unconducive for women but also not fit for the purpose of developing future leaders.

Given individualization as a key tenet of current society it not surprising that women often tend to individualize their experience in business school. A study on women on MBA programmes has for instance found that women did not think that the gender imbalance affected their own performance (JWT, 2005). Yet the same women also acknowledged that there were sexist undertones in class. The women in this study were adamant that they did not want to be singled out for special treatment. This special treatment might suggest that they were there not on merit but needed 'extra help' to succeed. This has to be understood in the context of post-feminism, in which it is assumed that gender inequality has either been eradicated or remains only marginally relevant for the experiences of women. Post-feminism takes as its starting point the assumption that feminism was so successful as a social movement that discourses for gender equality are no longer needed (Coppock, Haydon & Richter, 1995). Post-feminism can be understood as a historical move onward from something that comes after feminism but also an antithesis to and backlash against feminism (Gill, 2006). For Millennial women this means that they have been raised in a time when feminism was so successful that they feel that their choices are not affected by gender. Many Millennial women therefore seem to reject feminism as something that is no longer needed and they fail to recognize that much of their experience is still structured by gender (Scharff, 2011a). A similar move to ignore gender in business school will be traced in the empirical material of this chapter.

LAUNCHING YOURSELF

The rite of passage is a useful concept by which to understand career transitions in times when careers are said to become boundaryless. It is a particularly helpful concept when trying to understand the transition from a fairly junior person in an organization to a more senior position. For Millennials this is relevant first, because the boundaryless career means that they will have more rites of passage through their career and second, because they will develop from fairly junior persons in organizations to senior ones. The latter will provide insight into how leadership development can help this transition.

The first phase of the rite of passage is the separation from one's old life. Some of the stories that MBA students told us showed what motivated them to pursue an MBA. Emma, for instance, saw doing an MBA as a natural progression in her career. She worked as a consultant, and consultants are regularly charged to clients based on their educational level. Emma realized that she would not be able to rise through the ranks of her firm if she did not have an MBA. This would make her more valuable in the sense that she would fall into a higher category when it comes to charging clients. Through having an MBA, Emma would be able to command a higher fee level. In addition, doing an MBA would signal to her employer that she is keen to pursue a career and to move ahead. A higher fee level would also means that she would become more promotable. Reflecting the ideas entailed in the boundaryless carer, consultants seem to be evaluated based on their ability to sell their services on the market.

While for many like Emma doing an MBA meant progressing in the same firm, for others it was a way to circumvent particular barriers in their current career. Benjamin was working for an investment bank. He was happy with his job but he could not progress. His boss was just a few years older than him and would continue to run the 'desk' where he worked for the foreseeable future. Benjamin thought about looking for a similar position within the same investment bank and with others or he could enhance his skills elsewhere. He could either grow within or go elsewhere. Benjamin talked about enhancing his skills as a key mechanism through which he could progress faster. He decided that growing elsewhere would him expose to a range of new experiences that would be more beneficial for his career in the long run. In fact, after his MBA he joined another investment bank but was soon made redundant when investment banks were shrinking in order to cope with the contraction brought about by the economic crisis. However, he was able to find job with another investment bank shortly after, which he attributed to having the enhanced skills gained through his MBA degree.

Others like Matthieu talked about experiencing a career plateau. Matthieu has risen quickly in his job in the drinks industry in

France but felt that he could not progress any further. In addition, he was no longer excited about what he was doing and he thought about reigniting his passion for business through doing an MBA. Luke was even more critical about decisions to do an MBA, saying that you would not do an MBA if you are storming ahead in your original career. For him two years of doing a degree is a really long time, and the opportunity costs are huge because one not only has the expenses of school fees and maintenance, but one does also not earn an income for two years. If a person does well and is going to be promoted, this person would probably not do an MBA. The perspective that comes out here is that an MBA accelerates a career that is not quiet on track.

In light of these high opportunity costs, it was interesting to note that it was mainly women who talked about the skills they expected to pick up during an MBA degree. Frances, who is from South Africa, is a great example. She describes herself as not confident in her own abilities, and that doing an MBA would give her this confidence. Nadia, who is originally from Russia but has worked in London for a number of years, sees the MBA degree as giving her the soft skills that she needs to succeed as a leader in banking. Tanya similarly talked about the wish to grow herself by developing soft skills. After five years in a large company, she felt that the time was right to invest in herself. She had the time and the money and the lack of family obligations that allowed her to take this two-year break to develop herself. The MBA is therefore constructed as a way to re-launch one's career through an enhanced skill set. Most importantly, it also allowed the interviewees some 'me time' to take a step back from day-to-day work and broaden their horizons, meet new people and position themselves on the job market.

When MBA students talked about their experiences in business school, their accounts were very similar to what is described as liminality in the rite of passage. While this time was experienced as rich in influences, it was also experienced as unsettling. Emma, for instance, talked about how she changed her old patterns of behaviour. In school she was always very focused on her grades, but in business school the courses she picked were outside her comfort zone. She picked those courses to stretch herself rather than to get good grades. However, she found that there were many people who were much smarter in applying these skills than she was. While she did not feel stupid, she felt inexperienced. She could have decided to work extra hard to get the top marks. Instead, she realized that an MBA degree is much more about the experience than the grades. She did not want to sacrifice this special time in her life, when she basically had two years off work, and instead wanted to learn more from the interesting people to whom she was exposed. While she sometimes thought that other people were complete geniuses, she also realized that she was better than them at other things. She describes how she felt like being on a rollercoaster going up and down all the time. Some days she felt on top of the world, on other days she felt very down. Emma also referred to how she used the two years to find out which next career steps she wants to take and to figure out where her life is going. Others echoed this sentiment, such as Frances, who acknowledged that she and many others are trying to figure out where their place in the world is and that an MBA helps with this search. These are good descriptions of the unsettling effects of the transitional phase in a rite of passage.

The final phase of the rite of passage is characterized by stabilizing the new, carefully crafted identities that are emerging. This is the time when MBA students take stock and reflect on how they have changed and what have they learnt. Matthieu stressed that he took away two important things from business school: confidence and a powerful community. He also talked about how on leaving business school one is no longer a junior person but is transformed into someone more senior. In order to count as someone more senior it is important to use the currency of a strong brand. In this case, the business school fulfils the function of having a strong brand with which one can associate and which rubs off on the individual. Similarly Rafiq, who is of Middle Eastern origin, talked about how he will emerge from business school with a strong personal brand. For Rafiq a career is not a set of promotions in an organizational hierarchy but is marked by a chain of associations with strong brand names. The ability to have a successful boundaryless career thereby appears to depend on one's ability to associate oneself with recognisable brand names.

When Benjamin reflected on what he will take away from business school, he talked about his increased confidence and the right he had earned to be in a senior position. This senior position does not have to be in investment banking but can be any senior position. It appears that through earning an MBA one gains an entry ticket to count oneself as a senior leader. For Benjamin that not only manifests in being able to choose any professional setting, but moreover in the fact that he does no longer has to justify that he can do a job on a senior level. An MBA provides the symbolic power to occupy a more senior position without needing any further justification. This confidence expresses itself in the overall understanding of how business works. Kimi, who is from Asia, mentioned how the know-how of business gives her the confidence to master any business challenge. Frances talked for instance about how she now can read the *Financial Times* and understand it. 'Speaking business' fluently means that the rite of passage has been completed successfully.

Doing an MBA follows very much the phases of the rite of passage. It is evident that MBA students first decide to reshape their identities to make themselves fit for senior leadership positions and to advance in organizations. The MBA affords individuals the time and space to hone their skills and broaden their horizons. A strong community of people who go through the same stage at the same time provides a lot of support and opportunities to learn from one another. This strong community feeling binds people together in times of change. As the MBA students re-enter the workplace they have gained confidence, the association with a strong brand name and the ability to speak the language of business.

THE GENDERED CULTURE OF MBA EDUCATION

In the previous section, we have looked at how MBA students go through a rite of passage that leads them from being a junior person in an organization to potentially being a senior leader. Through this process the community was an important factor in shaping this transition. The notion of communitas takes this even further, because it argues that it homogenizes those who are in the liminal stage of the rite of passage (Turner, 1969). In a communitas people are equal and differences are made to disappear through the shared experience in the liminal stage. Markers of difference fall away or are ignored. This is similar to the ignorance of markers of difference encountered in individualization, where people believe themselves to be in charge of their own life regardless of their class, race or gender. This might appear contradictory, because individualism is often thought to refer to the fact that people are on their own and look out for themselves. However, in the sociological sense, we talk about a collective individualism in which people are united by the idea that they are individuals and free from markers of difference (Beck, 2000).

When we asked MBA students about the gender imbalance in business school, which was at this time below 30% of women, it was common to play down the importance of gender and say that it did not matter. This was achieved by stating that the scarcity of women in business school is just a function of business. Benjamin, for instance, said that business schools are a reflection of the business world where there are also few women. Vicente similarly stated that business is still a man's world but that this is slowly changing,

124

with more women becoming interested in business. Similarly, when I probed Emma if she thought it was problematic that most case studies are about men, she simply replied that this is just how the business world is and she was not bothered by it.

We also found that many MBA students described business as a game that is mainly played by men, and women should learn to play by their rules. Frances, for instance, states that 'Cause women don't do business, men do. So if you don't, if you want to do business, you have to learn to play business like a man'. Yatin also drew on the idea of business as being a game. He talked at length about the masculinity of business school, which was characterized for him by machismo and aggression. When we asked him how he saw his own role within this culture, he said that he was able to play this game even though he did not like it. However, he saw this 'macho camaraderie' as how business works. In order to join in one has to play the game.

Women also talked openly about how they sometimes felt excluded. Helen, for instance, talked about how her comments in group work are regularly ignored until a man says the same thing. She then described how she had had to learn to be more assertive and put her point across more forcefully. Helen adapted by learning the masculine skills that are required in business school and potentially also in a male-dominated business world. In tears, Dawn similarly talked about the sexist culture that she had encountered in business school. She cited as an example an incident of a classmate saying that women are in business to bring him coffee. However she relegated her experience to something she has to accept. Both Helen and Dawn talked about how one has to accept this masculine culture and the only thing one can do is to change your own behaviour.

Most MBA students also insisted that gender did not matter in business school (once one has accepted the overall masculine culture). When asked about how Caroline felt that three quarters of her fellow students were male, she said that she does not 'register' this fact. Caroline said that many things have fallen away for her in business such as gender. For instance, she no longer registers nationalities because she thinks they do not matter. The only thing that matters is if she can work with a person or not. Caroline asserted that she only judges people based on competence and merit, which is not unlike the comments regularly made by dominant groups when they talk about minority groups by referring to the discourse of merit. Andrew, for instance, stated that he would not mind if there were more women in business school, so long as the school ensured that they were there on merit. Thereby he implicitly suggests a potential quota for women in business schools which is seen as contradicting inclusion on for the basis of merit. Rafiq similarly commented that a quota for women would not be in the interest of business schools at all, implying that this would lower the merit.

Gender is said to fall away in business school because people are there on merit and bond on this basis. Focusing on gender is perceived as breaking the communitas that is carefully constructed as part of the liminal stage of the rite of passage. This becomes particularly visible in regard to the Women in Business Club. The purpose of this club is to build networks. The Women in Business Club eschews any association with being feminist. The club provides what one interviewee, Peggy, called 'preferential access' to recruiters from consultancies and investment banks via such events as women-only breakfasts. For women students, membership seemed almost compulsory but few described themselves as active.

Nadia joined the Women in Business Club and clearly sees a need to help women juggle their different roles in business. Yet she hates the idea of constructing men and women as different. A similar sentiment is voiced by Caroline. She talked about how a group of female friends in business school is a useful network for her to consider how she might be able to combine work and family, but she said that this informal group would not discuss things like the glass ceiling and gender discrimination. She also has what she called an allergic reaction to the club, which is too big and too organized for her. Caroline thinks it borders on whining. Carrying derogatory connotations of being childish, complaining, fault-finding and irritable, the accusation of 'whining' is often levelled at women's groups, particularly those that are seen as feminist (Phipps, 2006). Caroline thereby distances herself from anything that could be seen as feminist. She thinks that those women complain about the glass ceiling and the like, but Caroline insists that she never saw a glass ceiling when she worked. Caroline here mobilizes the glass ceiling to argue that it does not exist. Yet at the fairly junior level that she had in the organization prior to entering business school, she might not have experienced it. This allows her to present the world of work as gender equal, and to claim that gender no longer matters.

Caroline's concern about too much being made of any disadvantages women might face was echoed in the interview with Frances, who had worked in a very male-dominated industry. Frances describes herself as 'nervous around women'. She explains this by saying that women and minorities often cause their own problems in the workplace. While she accepts that there is some sexism, in many cases what women experience as sexism is just part of working hard. For her, crying discrimination every time something does not go well for a woman is short-sighted because there might be other reasons that can account for this experience. Such behaviour is nourished in Frances' view by institutions like the Women in Business Club, which allow women to describe their experience in regard to sexism. Frances maintains that gender discrimination will not always play a role. She goes on to imply that women have to toughen up instead of complaining about gender discrimination all the time. By becoming tough and assertive women will not only learn to fit in in business schools but also in business. They will become leaders who follow more stereotypically masculine traits because this is how one succeeds. Not only are women socialized away from femininity in business school, but so too are men. The ideal leader produced by business schools is still more masculine than feminine. This means that neither women nor men will learn to value stereotypically feminine types of behaviour, which are particularly important in a business world in which being a coaching manager is central.

So why were women MBA students reluctant to acknowledge how gender shapes their experiences? For them, acknowledging that gender matters counteracts individualization because it means that MBA students are not masters of their own destiny. By investing in an MBA one expects to succeed in business as a result, and questioning the gender neutrality of the workplace would mean an implicit acknowledgement that doing an MBA might have been not such a good investment.

Moreover, the communitas of the liminal stage requires men and women to ignore any markers of difference because these would indicate that they are not a homogenous group. However, ignoring difference allows them to create the impression of a homogenous group that collectively finds its place in the world. Any formal statements of difference would break this unity. However, this difference sometimes breaks through informally, with women discussing the support they gain through informal groups of female MBA students. Getting together to discuss their CVs or how to combine having a relationship with a career was described by women as a refuge and a support network. However, these attempts to discuss difference have to remain informal to protect the community of MBA students in the rite of passage.

LEARNING TO BE INCLUSIVE LEADERS

The centrality of learning for Millennials not only extends to on the job learning; formal learning retains its importance. As we have seen by looking at MBA education, an MBA in particular helps individuals to manage status transitions from being a junior person in an organization to potentially being a more senior person. For this a rite of passage is important. The first stage consists of detaching oneself from one's previous identity. This often involves explaining why one has embarked on an MBA. This commonly involves a wish for progression either within the company or industry, or a career change. In the liminal stage, individuals develop and form new identities. This stage is often experienced as daunting but also empowering. Finally, the newly minted MBA students prepare to take leadership positions in business. The transition from being a junior to being a potentially senior person in business is completed.

The rite of passage is not only relevant for MBA education but for formal education in general. Most courses and degrees evolve across a similar arc. It could be argued that in the age of the boundaryless career, the rite of passage becomes even more constant and is not only a ritual completed at one point in time but has to be continually undergone in order to keep learning. This would mean that the requirement to constantly learn either formally or on the job means that the three-part rite of passage becomes a phenomenon that has to be completed time and time again. However, some rites of passage, like doing an MBA, will stand out as central and will ensure that identity transformations are secured through formal education.

Of particular importance to formal education is the communitas that develops in the liminal phase among the participants. This is important because it facilitates learning among students. Organizations can use this strategically in their talent development programmes, and in fact many organizations already do this. Building a community feeling among graduates, for instance, is a very important way to create networks. Those networks can be used to provide feedback to young professionals not only on their work but also on their new identities. As discussed in the previous section, feedback is something Millennials crave to improve themselves and they are open to receiving peer feedback.

However, the intense communitas that evolves during the rite of passage also means that any forms of difference are downplayed and ignored. We have seen this in relation to gender issues during the MBA education. Standing out as different would break the community feeling and is perceived to create separation. This ignoring of gender is not only a function of a repudiated feminism, although that plays a role, but is also a way to maintain community. It is also an attempt to justify the investment made in an MBA, because Millennial women do not want to perceive this in their education as wasted because their status as women means that they will not be equal in the workplace.

Discussing difference is important for both Millennial women and men to make sense of their experience, and organizations would do well to create ways to encourage this reflection, which seems to have little space in business schools. While formal women's networks are often rejected as too formalized, too separatist and as drawing too much attention to gender, it transpired that informal networks of women are a useful way of establishing support.

With difference silenced, aspiring managers will not learn anything about how to manage a diverse workforce. They will not have the tools to manage inclusively. Instead they are going to reproduce a traditional leadership style, which relies on the emulation of a single norm. The silencing of difference in MBA degrees influences the type of leader that business schools develop. We have seen that women try to emulate the competitiveness and instrumentality they observe in their male peers. They talked about the need to be assertive and to toughen up. Women thereby show gender flexibility in taking up attributes, skills and behaviours more commonly associated with men. Yet the future workplace will require them to be coaching managers who nurture their teams and connect with customers and stakeholders through listening. These are skills associated not with masculinity but rather femininity. Those feminine skills have little room in business schools and the ideal that MBA students emulate is that of a tough, instrumental and competitive manager. While women have adopted masculine skills, we do not see a revaluation of feminine skills in formal education. Men need to develop gender flexibility and start to enact skills associated with femininity, and women need to learn that femininity can be an asset in management. Organizations therefore need to ensure that feminine skills are developed early on in leaders to avoid the next generation of leaders seeing the ideal as more masculine than feminine. Instead both gendered skills are required to be a successful manager.

SIGNATURE PRACTICE: ALTERNATIVE APPROACHES TO DELIVERING MBA PROGRAMMES

The disappearance of gender in many business schools often leads to questions of whether single-sex education might be a solution to overcome this situation. One of the few places where women can gain an MBA in a single-sex environment is Simmons College in Boston, Massachusetts. The women-only MBA was set up in 1975 and has since then delivered an MBA programme that is designed to equip women with the right competencies and competence (Simmons, 2012). The MBA curriculum follows the fairly standard lines that one would expect from an MBA programme. The difference is that it is delivered by female and male faculty, with women in mind. At Simmons, case studies featuring women as protagonists and female guest speakers are the norm. Rather than being in a minority position, which often leads to the wish to disguise the impact of gender, at Simmons women are the norm. This is said to produce confident women who are ready to take leadership positions in business.

The counterargument provided by mainstream MBA programmes to women-only MBAs is the fact that women have to manage in gender diverse environments. Having a single-sex education might be less suited to developing the skills that are needed in mixed-sex environments. Moreover, this also means that only women will learn about the importance of gender diversity. If mainstream programmes remain unchanged, future managers will not learn how to manage gender diversity.

However, mainstream programmes have been resistant to putting gender on the table as a topic for reflecting on the development of competence. Unless these programmes are changing fundamentally in terms of curriculum and atmosphere, there seems to be value in educating women in single-sex environments to be leaders. At Simmons women do follow a standard MBA programme, but they also learn that gender might affect their future careers and they develop strategies for dealing with that. Participants of the all-female MBA have reported how useful they found the experience of being educated in a single-sex environment and how it has set them up for a successful career.

CONCLUSION

In this chapter we have explored how formal education transforms identities through a rite of passage. These rites of passage are going to be more common for Millennials, who have to reinvent themselves constantly. These rites of passage ensure that new identities can be formed in a safe environment. In the process strong bonds emerge, which are called a communitas. People within this community will learn from one another and become a prime way through which feedback is shared. However, these strong communities also mean that difference is systematically ignored and silenced. Talking about being a woman is, for instance, seen as potentially damaging to the community by drawing attention to difference. Gender, as well as any other forms of difference, are therefore ignored. This means that future leaders do not learn to manage diversity and to be inclusive leaders. This becomes apparent in the fact that women in business school learn to embody masculinity by being competitive, tough and instrumental. However, the feminine skills that are needed to be a coaching manager who provides constructive feedback and develops individuals and engages stakeholders are ignored. Men and women need to start displaying those skills to ensure that they will be leaders who are fit for the future.

9

VISIBILITY — THE POLITICS OF NETWORKING AND APPEARANCE

INTRODUCTION

Lauren decided to go to a women's network meeting in her organization. She had been invited to similar events several times before but had never gone. However, on that day she thought that it might be useful to meet some other women, particularly senior ones, to enhance her career. She was currently working on an intensive project and arrived at the meeting at the last minute in a great rush. The event started with a talk by a female fashion designer who talked about what to wear and not to wear at work. Lauren immediately felt self-conscience about how she was dressed. Maybe she should have worn the new smart shift dress with heels as the guest speaker suggested instead of her old and by now ill-fitting trouser suits with a flowery shirt and her worn ballet flats? Then the guest speaker moved on to talk about accessories and professional hair, and again Lauren became conscious that she had been too tired the night before to blow-dry her hair carefully. It was falling naturally in a slight wave, which was a far cry from the chic, professionally blow-dried hair that the guest speaker characterized as professional. Lauren wondered how she should find time to get her hair blow-dried while working ten-hour days with an hour commute at either end and a non-existent lunch break. She had problems finding time to eat and her hair was not her main concern. The guest speaker moved on to talk about make-up, which should not be visible, and fingernails that should be well groomed but not painted in strong colours. Looking at her fingernails, Lauren asked herself if the slight lilac colour she had chosen to paint her nails with was neutral enough.

Feeling completely out of place due to her appearance was not a good start to the networking session over drinks and nibbles that followed. There was no one there she knew. She noticed that there were some senior women who she wanted to connect with. All the senior women were standing together. Laura plucked up her courage and decided to stand next to the group of senior women. She waited for a good opportunity to introduce herself, but one did not arise. The senior women seemed concerned with one another and did not even look at Lauren. Lauren decided to contribute to the conversation and made a funny remark, which was completely ignored by the group of women. After around 15 minutes of standing silently with the group, three of the four women excused themselves as they had to go back to work or had to go home. The final senior woman looked at Lauren and Lauren thought that this was great because she now could engage the senior woman. However the senior woman just looked at her and moved to talk to the fashion designer without even excusing herself.

Lauren looked around the room and noticed that there were groups of senior women and groups of junior women. There was no group for mid-level women managers, who were staggeringly absent from the meeting. After being ignored by the group of senior women, Lauren decided to join a group of junior women. This group at least gave her the opportunity to introduce herself. The conversation centred around the fashion designer's talk. The junior women felt that they should be allowed to wear whatever they want at work. They wanted to be themselves and not comply with norms of professional dress that have been developed a long time ago. They thought that the workplace has moved on from this and that old-fashioned dress codes are no longer important. Most of the women were attending a women's networking event for the first time but they said they were not likely to go to another event. Lauren left and was at least happy to have found some like-minded junior women. She thought that she might meet them again informally.

While many senior women want to be supportive of their junior colleagues, Lauren's example shows that the reality often looks different. Lauren's story combines not only her experiences with women's networks but also indicates the importance of appearance for women in organizations. It illustrates the elements of visibility that are experienced by Millennial women as they develop into leaders. In this chapter, the focus will be on exploring the importance of visibility for leadership development from a gender perspective.

VISIBILITY – A DOUBLE-EDGED SWORD FOR WOMEN LEADERS

For most aspiring leaders, getting exposure is centrally important to their leadership journey. Exposure gained through working on business-critical assignments helps them to stand out. For women, visibility is not a problem. In male-dominated environments in particular women often stand out as unusual. Enhanced visibility and associated performance pressures come part and parcel with being a token (Kanter, 1977). The pressures on women to perform well not only stem from the enhanced visibility that they have as minorities in leadership positions. These pressures might be exacerbated by the fact that research evidence suggests that women are also more likely to be put into high-risk senior leadership positions (Ryan & Haslam, 2005). This phenomenon is called the glass cliff and denotes that women are more likely to be appointed to senior positions in organizations if the organization is not doing well. This in turn increases the risk of failure in a leadership position.

Why is this enhanced visibility problematic? It is often assumed that learning through mistakes is a central feature of developing as a leader. In a previous chapter, we discussed the role of experiential learning for developing leaders. Part of this experiential learning is being able to learn from mistakes. However, in order to be able to do this, one must feel that one is working in an environment where mistakes are not frowned upon but seen as ways to learn. In the academic literature such an environment is often described through the notion of psychological safety. This is a team level construct that measures how far team members feel that their team offers them a safe environment for interpersonal risk taking (Edmondson, 1999). It has been shown that successful leaders create psychological safety in their teams, develop trust within teams and facilitate learning from failures (Edmondson, 2003; Carmeli, Tishler & Edmondson, 2012). Although there is only limited research on the importance of making mistakes to develop as a leader, it can be expected that having psychological safety in their immediate environment is very important to aspiring leaders to facilitate learning from failure and mistakes. However, with women having token higher visibility, it might be the case that they have less opportunity to learn from failures and mistakes.

The increased visibility of women often finds its expression in discussions on what women are supposed to wear at work. While it appears that women have too much visibility at times, they do seem to have not the right kind of visibility. Women do not shine due to their performance. They shine because they are a minority and because of the way they dress. Visibility therefore means different things for men and women. For men it means standing out from a sea of similar men, and is commonly accomplished through performance and networking. Women have automatic visibility due to their minority position and a focus on dress, yet they are more likely to be put into positions where the risk of failure is high.

Let's take a look at the dynamics of networking and appearance at work. Networking is one of the mechanisms through which visibility can be gained. It is in fact common to assert that having the right types of networks is essential to succeeding in organizations. Research has also shown that men and women have different types of networks. Women have wider networks in organizations, which is largely the result of being in a minority (Ibarra, 1992). It is presumed that we like to associate with people who are more like us. This is called homophily, and is a concept we have explored in a previous chapter. Homophily can express itself in relation to gender, class and race, as well as other dimensions in which similarity can be perceived. Education, such as having graduated from the same university, is for instance one element that leads people to bond. Similarly, shared values and beliefs bond people together, which can for instance be observed in people who follow similar religious beliefs.

As there are few women in many organizations, particularly higher up the organizational ladder, the theory of homophily suggests that women will bond with other women. As women cannot find many women in close proximity, their networks are wider. Curiously, the different network structures of men and women have consequences for performance. Research exploring star investment bankers has, for instance, found that while men lose their star performance when moving companies, women do not (Groysberg, 2008). This is the case because female star performers have wider networks that exist outside the company whereas men tend to have networks within the company, which they lose once they move. The networks of female star performers are portable due to the different network structures.

This however does not change the fact that many women perceive the 'old boys' network' as hindering their career. The secret weapon that many organizations deploy to counteract the old boy's network is women's networks. In theory women's networks should equip women with a sense of collective power that they can use as a leverage to transform organizations. This is in conflict, however, with the findings of a research study on women's experience and the perceived career benefits from an internal women's network (Bierema, 2005). This study indicates that many women fear that participating in such a network is career damaging. Women in the study did not want to be seen to challenge the dominant culture. Even though awareness raising for gendered power relations is seen as another benefit of women's networks, the women in this study have varying degrees of gender awareness and were often not willing to act on inequalities they encountered out of fear of being seen as a 'troublemaker'.

The study shows that the network has little impact on changing the overall culture in the organization, which was not favourable to women. The homophily of the network, supported by the fact that the women shared the same gender and organizational culture, meant that the network did not profit from external input. External input is known to enrich networks. It is therefore suggested that network members are varied and networks are opened to people from outside the organization. In addition, men were not involved in the women's network and the onus was put on women to change the organization. This is problematic because men determine the majority culture. It is therefore vital that the culture of the organization, management and the network itself is gender conscious.

Women's networks are also often associated with being feminist. As we have already seen, feminism is no longer something with which many women identify. Feminism is something for which the grandmothers and mothers of these young women have fought, but for many younger women fighting for gender equality is no longer seen as needed because gender equality is thought to have been achieved. Younger women still experience traces of gender inequality in the workplace, but the sense-making processes around those gender inequalities have changed (Scharff, 2011a). Young women perceive themselves as the agents of their own destiny.

In such an individualized world in which Millennial women grew up, women's networks are easily understood as antiquated and no longer needed. We have seen that in the previous chapter, when the ambivalent relationship to the Women in Business Club in the business school setting was discussed. If you no longer think in categories of men and women, or claim not to do so, then having a women's network is not an idea that will appeal to many young women. In addition, women's networks often do not help Millennial women develop networks with senior women. In fact in many cases women's networks only lead to more ambivalent attitudes towards senior women, which we have discussed in relation to role models. For Millennial women traditional women's networks might therefore be less well suited to developing their visibility with senior leaders.

Most people would agree that there are specific dress codes in every workplace. For instance if you are working for Google casual clothing is the norm, whereas for bankers a suit is required in order to appear professional. In academic terms we talk about the 'aesthetic labour' that is required from individuals in order to perform a professional identity. Dress is also used as a symbolic demarcation line between men and women. In many restaurants and airlines, for instance, men and women wear different types of uniform. In professional contexts the suit is a common tool for men to convey professionalism. Research has argued, for instance, that by wearing a suit the individual bodies of men disappear behind a common cloak (Hollander, 1994). For a customer this means that regardless of whom they meet, they feel a consistency in service.

In contrast, for women dress is a bit more complex. Women have to convey their femininity through dress. At the same time they should not appear too feminine because this would mean departing too much from the masculine ideal worker norm. As with their general behaviour, women have to bolster their femininity so as to appear as women while also furnishing their masculinity so as to appear to fulfil the ideal worker norm. This often means wearing the feminine version of the masculine suit, while avoiding appearing too sexual (e.g. skirt length) or too feminine (e.g. salmon-coloured or flowery prints) (Entwistle, 2000).

While the trouser suit will be an option for Millennial men to appear professional, dress is not as clear cut for Millennial women and there is a fine line between something that is perceived as acceptable and something that is seen as unacceptable. This might explain why for many women's networks discussing dress code and appearance is on the agenda; they can gain knowledge about the types of dress that are acceptable in their organizational setting and, if they are interested in fashion, might also derive pleasure from discussing clothing. However, if one is a Millennial woman for whom gender is no longer a category that they register, and for whom authenticity is important, they are not only hesitant to join women in the first place, but will also find it strange to talk about dress at work. However, their appearance alongside their networks will influence their visibility.

MILLENNIAL WOMEN'S EXPERIENCES OF WOMEN'S NETWORKS

Women's networks came up regularly when we talked with the Millennials about gender at work. The wish of Millennial women to be authentic, together with increased individualization means that women's networks are not a natural place for Millennial women to gain support. The reason women's networks were brought up by some Millennial women was due to the fact that they had made specific experiences in those groups. In addition, women's networks were one of the few instances where they saw gender being the focus of attention. They therefore often drew on their experiences of women's networks when discussing gender at work.

Tina is a typical example of the kind of stories we heard about women's networks. She described that when she started at her company, she heard about a women's network that the company supports. Tina was careful to state that she prefers to experience something first before judging or talking badly about it. This sentence alone makes it explicit that the experience she was about to recount was not a positive one. The topic of the evening was what to wear at work. She thought that this was an interesting topic; however, she then learned that women are not supposed to wear cardigans at work because cardigans do not help them exert authority. She was the only person in the room wearing a cardigan. Men in her area of work wear cardigans. Tina could not see why she should not wear a cardigan at work and, not surprisingly, did not agree with the 'no cardigan' rule. Tina felt offended by the assertion that she should not wear a cardigan because she could see men wearing cardigans and could not see anything wrong with this.

Tina continued to explain that she felt that the women she met at the networking event were really focusing on the wrong things. For her, networks do play a role when there is harassment and bullying, which she appreciates can happen. However, she is careful not to look for those issues. This discursive move is similar to what we have seen in the business school setting, where some women almost implied that women and minorities look for instances of discrimination. In a sense, Tina seems to suggest that when focusing on those issues one is likely to over-interpret one's experience. Tina continued by providing an example for what she sees as over-interpreting. She spoke about a woman during the networking meeting who recounted that a man complimented her on her outfit and she understood this as harassment. For Tina, this woman was jumping to conclusions. She felt that the man might have wanted to be sensitive, attentive and friendly by giving a compliment.

Tina then mentioned that another woman at the meeting said that she felt excluded because the men in her team talked about football. Tina said that this woman should have started a conversation about something else, like a book, a film or even shopping, in which she has an interest. For Tina this is not a gender thing but it is a matter of fact that people like different things. Tina claims that she knows many women who are passionate about football, which is why talking about football is not exclusionary. What we see here is that this experience, which can be read as gendered, is seen as individual rather than an example of gender differences.

Interestingly, Tina then started to talk about things that she was surprised to find in the workplace. She thought that after all these diversity campaigns discrimination would not happen today anymore and she said how difficult she finds it to deal with those incidents. The incidents she recounts are a person not answering the phone to her presumably because she is a woman, or when she has to present in a conference call, she is sometimes put on hold and not listened to. When she encounters these things, she always asks herself if it is she who is doing something wrong. Therefore she searches for the fault in her own behaviour rather than looking for systemic gender inequality. Tina continues to state that she sees herself as lucky because she is in a graduate cohort and she has never experienced pay discrepancies between men and women. While Tina sometimes experiences what can be seen as gender discrimination, she is always careful to explore what is happening in the situation rather than jumping to the conclusion that this must be due to gender. Her experience in the women's network, however, was that this network used a narrow frame of reference by thinking that every situation they are in happens because of their gender.

Grace describes her experience of joining a women's networking dinner as strange. Only three women at the meeting were junior in the organization, including herself. Everyone else was older and more senior. Older for Grace meant being over 40 years of age. She describes how she could not connect to those women who were much older and at different life stages. Most of them had children, some of whom were even grown-up, which meant that they had very different interests and wanted to work on different things. Grace therefore did not really feel at home at this women's dinner.

Kim also talked about her thoughts on women's networking meeting. For Kim women's networking meetings are a way to help women network. In Kim's view men know how to network and make decisions while networking. She recounts that when she attended a meeting that should have been to help women network, the example of making decisions while playing golf was used. For her this was not malicious in the sense that women are ruled out. In Kim's view women just do not play golf, and as a consequence they are not part of the decision-making process. Kim says that she knows some women who have started to play golf to be part of this decision-making. Kim believes this to be a very clever strategy. What we see here is that the role of women is to make themselves relevant and visible by adopting and emulating behaviour they see in men in order to avoid being excluded. We see that the culture of making decisions while playing golf is not questioned and it is just seen as a matter for women to learn to fit in.

It appears difficult for Millennial women to make sense of gender in the workplace when it affects them negatively. What we have seen before is that they mainly look for a fault in themselves and modify their behaviour to fit in. This is not dissimilar to what we have seen in the business school environment. It indicates that gender is something that most women agree might play a role, but they struggle to see when it matters and when it does not. For them women's networks often use one-dimensional ways of making sense, seeing gender as the only important parameters. For Millennial women, this means ignoring others ways through which a situation might be seen.

STANDING OUT – THE ADVANTAGES OF BEING A WOMAN

Rather than experiencing gender as something negative, many Millennial women we talked to spoke about the advantages of being a woman: one stands out more. Kareena, who has a Chinese background, said that being a woman is clearly an advantage. This is due to the paucity of women in senior positions, which leads to the fact that many organizations try to encourage women to move up the organizational ladder. Kareena also said that women stand out straight away and she will be remembered because most of her colleagues are men. Being a woman and being different allows an individual to stand out and gain additional visibility. However, Kareena acknowledges that standing out can be risky too: if she says something right, she gets the credit; if she says something wrong, people will think that this 'girl is just a bit stupid'. Kareena notices here that the increased visibility of women can work in their favour or against them. This puts special performance pressure on those women who stand out tokenistically (Kanter, 1977). It also indicates that learning through mistakes as part of their leadership development will be more difficult.

Imelda voiced a similar thought. Imelda is ambitious and is open with her manager about her ambitions. Her manager has told her that she will be able to move into a leadership position quickly because she is a woman and there are not enough women in leadership positions. Imelda had never thought about gender being an advantage before, but now it appears to her that being a woman is an extra help if she wants to progress. While she claims never to have experienced negative gender or age discrimination, she has also never experienced this type of positive discrimination first-hand. However, she thinks that being a woman might be of extra help once she advances in the organization.

Leela also reflected on the fact that it might be an advantage to be a woman. She told us about a conversation she had with a male colleague, who suggested that women have it easier because they can just smile and get their way. For Leela that is unprofessional and she hates the idea that people might just help her because she has smiled at them. She wants to believe that she is in the company because of her talent and not because she has a nice smile. To justify the opinion of her colleague she said that he was working with a girl who uses her looks to advance in the organization. However, for Leela that too is very unprofessional because she wants to be recognized for her talent and not because she is attractive. What is suggested here is the idea that women can use their sexual attractiveness to influence men, a notion that was immediately repudiated as unprofessional. It is also interesting to note how in the previous two examples it is men who seem to advise their female colleagues that they have an advantage because they are women.

This visibility also became apparent in a story that Christine told us. For Christine gender does not matter much, and she wants to behave like her male colleagues. However, her additional visibility as a woman means that she sometimes confronts boundaries. She recounts a story in which she was working a project in Vietnam. In order to get from the hotel to the company, the consultants had to use taxis. There were two options: either the hotel taxis or the local taxis. The hotel taxis were ten times more expensive than the local taxis. Christine noticed that all of her male colleagues used local taxis and she decided to do the same to save the company some money. Christine describes her shock and surprise when she was called by the head office and told in not unclear terms that she cannot use local taxis because of her security. Christine understands that women are more vulnerable. However, she was surprised by the extent to which the company went to protect her. While she would have understood this during the dark, she found it surprising that she was unable to use a local taxi during daytime. This was for her a clear incident when she was treated differently. While gender was not conceptualized here as an advantage it was nevertheless seen as a way by which women can stand out. It also shows that different 'rules' often apply to men and women.

Rather than talking about gender as something negative, these examples from the interviews show that in many cases women saw it as a potential advantage to be female and that one has to comply to special rules as a woman. This is due to the fact that women can stand out as a minority in most business situations and therefore have higher levels of recognisability with colleagues and clients. However, this standing out comes part and parcel with the fact that that their actions are also under scrutiny. This in turn makes it difficult for women to learn through mistakes. Any mistakes they make will be as visible as they are.

DRESSING THE PART

We also found that dress and appearance was another theme discussed in relation to gender at work. A good example of this is provided by Ian. When asked whether or not he sees any gender difference in his workplace, he denies it and says that there is not a huge amount of difference – apart from how people dress. In his view the maddest a man can dress is to wear a different type of tie. For him, women in contrast have more latitude as they are able to wear different things, even open shoes. In his view anything passes for a woman. What Ian notices is that for men a suit and tie are the standard uniform, which does not allow much variation apart from the tie. For him, women can pick their clothing from a range of options without being conspicuous. Lyndon echoed this by saying that in terms of dress code women are allowed to get away with much more.

Stefan also discussed appearance in his interview. He told us a story about how he saw the female CEO of a well-known company in a video. He noticed that she was wearing jewellery that produced a clinging sound every time she moved. For Stefan that meant that she was using her femininity as a positive element. Instead of trying to appear like a man, which for him means wearing trousers and using a dark voice, this woman was happy to flaunt her femininity. Stefan asserts that women adopt this masculine type of behaviour when they fear not being able to bring a point across or not being taken seriously. He continued to talk about two of his female managers, whom he describes as 'girls' before correcting himself by stating that they are female managers. These female managers are also in his view very much women and they are feminine, which for him means wearing dresses. Being feminine is for Stefan how women should be in the workplace. This example illustrates how dress and appearance become an example for how femininity and masculinity are performed in the workplace.

Jewellery was also discussed by Kimi, one of the MBA students, when discussing an image that showed a young women walking down the street in Central London. The woman was wearing a thick gold necklace with a skirt suit and for Kimi that is unprofessional. Kimi states that the woman looks like going off to party rather than working. Similarly, Emma commented on the attire of this woman by saying that her skirt is very short. When I asked Emma if she found this inappropriate she stated that it shows that the woman is confident. For Emma the woman is not hiding the fact that she is feminine and 'at the same time' powerful. The use of 'at the same time' indicates that normally femininity and power do not go well together. However, for Emma the image shows that femininity can go together with being powerful. In addition, Emma states that this confident feminine woman shows that she can afford nice things (like the gold necklace) through working in a male-dominated environment. For Emma this is an empowering image.

Other MBA students also talked about appropriate dress at work. Ulrike, for instance, talked about the importance of dressing in such a way that clients can respect you. This means dressing in a neutral way, which includes, for instance, avoiding very pink lipstick. For her it is important that nothing catches the client's eye, and so allow a complete focus on the business problem. For Ulrike this means toning down femininity by wearing appropriately neutral lipstick to avoid irritating the client. Having the wrong kind of lipstick is thus equated with the wrong type of visibility.

While there were some references to men wearing suits and ties, the attire of men did not regularly attract much comment from the Millennials we spoke to. For women, in contrast, dress and what not to wear at work was often the focus of attention. The aforementioned examples illustrate the intricacies and pitfalls that exist in the appropriate appearance for women. Above all they show the different interpretations that Millennials have of appearance. While the dress 'rules' for men seem straightforward, finding the right attire for women seems to be more flexible and subject to interpretation. This shows the struggle that women have to go through to find the right type of visibility.

THE RIGHT TYPE OF VISIBILITY

Visibility is very important in inspiring leaders, and creating visibility with the right type of people is going to be crucial for Millennials and particularly Millennial women. Visibility often translates into having the right type of network. One of the common reasons why women do not advance is that they lack the right type of networks. To remedy this issue, many organizations support internal women's networks. These are thought to provide women with support from other women and an opportunity for them to discuss issues that are relevant to them. However, many Millennial women are sceptical about women's networks. Some Millennial women do not feel welcome in those networks or dislike the idea that there are behavioural rules to which they as women in business have to comply. In addition, many Millennial women perceive these women's networks as using oversimplified explanations that only centre around gender. Millennial women, with their individualized mindsets, are likely to reject explanations of their experience that construct them as recipients of discrimination.

What does this mean for practice? Are women's networks obsolete? Women's networks have a place in organizations but they are not a panacea for developing women as leaders. In order to be effective women's networks need to ensure that they are inclusive and do not exclude or marginalize junior women, as in the example with which we began this chapter. This can be done by encouraging senior women to spend time with junior women. In addition, more multifaceted interpretations of reality need to be offered. Younger women need to learn when gender matters and when it does not, and they need to find their own ways of addressing this through strategies with which they feel comfortable. Women's networks are only going to be effective when they create a gender-conscious climate, but it is exactly this gender-conscious climate that repels many Millennial women because they believe it leads to a reductionist view of reality.

One way to overcome the rejection of women's network groups is to broaden their membership to include men. It is possible to invite senior and mid-level men to network meetings. This lends support to the internal importance of women's networks and allows women to gain visibility with men who are more likely to decide over their promotion. Such an approach will also ensure that men learn about how women experience gender at work. Men are often powerful allies in driving the gender-change agenda forward, and by excluding them from women's networks, the issue of gender is positioned as something that only concerns women and not men. This approach is short-sighted because men are needed to help change the organizational culture. They can do this if they have an awareness of the issues women confront.

It is possible to create a network around other identity categories such as being Millennials or new starters in an organization. Millennials can then talk about their experiences at work. It is important for those groups to be gender-balanced, which will ensure that issues of gender are discussed without making them too formal. Calling it something else creates much less resistance from Millennial women towards these networks. Millennial men will also learn a great deal about gender, which will ensure that they become inclusive leaders. Again it is important that these networks gain expose to senior leaders so as to give Millennials visibility. A casual and playful engagement with gender in an organization will best engage Millennials in those issues that they often perceive as long solved.

SIGNATURE PRACTICE: BUDDYING UP – DEVELOPING NETWORKS

One way to increase visibility for women is through women's networks, but Millennial women are often a bit resistant to joining such networks. A different approach would be to focus on other dimensions of diversity such as generation and/or age. This works particularly well if one considers other dimensions around which Millennials can bond, such as being a new joiner in an organization. In order to allow new joiners to build networks and settle into the organizational culture, Cassidian piloted a 'buddy network'. Cassidian, part of the European Aeronautic Defence and Space Company (EADS), is providing defence and security solutions globally and is headquartered in the South of Germany.

The buddy network meant that new joiners were matched with people who had worked in the organization for up to three years and thus might still remember how it felt to join the organization themselves. New joiners were matched with people who worked in different functional areas. Although gender was included as a parameter in the matching process, it was not foregrounded to the participants. The small pilot project brought together 18 individuals in nine pairs for a six-month programme. Out of these 18 individuals, five buddies were women and one newcomer was a woman.

The aim of the initiative was to keep the relationships fairly informal and allow the participants to structure the relationship in a way that works for them. The participants made great use of this freedom. In addition, to the pair interactions, the group was also encouraged to meet over a weekly lunch in the canteen. This offering was taken up quickly and ensured that relationships beyond the buddy pair were created. The group also took the initiative to organize various other events themselves, such as visits to each other's workplaces.

The comments received throughout stressed how much the individuals profited from the buddy relationship, and they

145

specifically enjoyed the visibility that the programme gave them beyond their immediate work environment. Even though the programme is a small pilot it indicates how visibility in an organization can be fostered by creating networks for individuals across boundaries. By including tenure in the organization, functional area and gender parameters in the matching process it was ensured that the networks created are diverse.

While Millennials often think that inequality is a thing of the past, they need to be given the right tools with which to analyse their experience. An example of one of my students illustrates this well. Charlize participated in my diversity and inclusion module. Reflecting on her experience she told me that she never thought that gender would be an issue for her. However, having explored the different dimensions of diversity and how they manifest in the workplace, she reflected on her own experience at university. In her first year, she was working in a group with only men. As the only woman the group assigned her the secretarial role. She did not think much of it at the time and just did it. Only after doing my module, she realized that she had complied with a stereotype about women. Instead of taking notes she would have preferred to work on the 'big ideas' that the group had. Charlize devised a strategy to avoid similar situations in the future. She was keen to subvert gender stereotypes because this would allow her to follow her passion for strategy. As this example illustrates, it is important to integrate these reflections in training. They will not only ensure that gender-sensitivity is developed but also that Millennial men and women learn more about themselves. This will ensure that they develop into reflective leaders for whom managing inclusively has become second nature.

SIGNATURE PRACTICE: CREATING VISIBILITY THROUGH NETWORKING AND SHORTLISTING

General Electric (GE), the multinational conglomerate famously founded by Thomas Edison, is a company that values innovation for driving change. Inclusiveness is one of GE's guiding leadership values. Its high potential leaders are developed through the leadership ranks on the basis of performance and values, which form the cornerstone of GE's culture. However, inclusiveness can mean different things in different areas of the world.

Gender inclusivity is often seen as particularly challenging in the Middle East, Northern Africa and Turkey (MENAT) region. GE in MENAT has realized that an increasing part of its current and future talent pool in this emerging region is constituted by women. Yet different gender regimes in countries as diverse as Turkey and Saudi Arabia make it difficult to develop a standardized approach to including this diverse talent. Women in this region are often well educated, and those that have decided to be in the workforce are driven to grow as professionals and as leaders. GE in MENAT therefore embarked on a journey to create an environment in which women in particular can flourish and contribute to innovation and business growth. The tools used for this include a mix of flexible working arrangements, a women's network, a review of all maternity polices and a structured personalized development plan for more than 20 of the best next generation female talents.

In addition, GE MENAT is using two tools to create visibility for women in the MENAT region: encouraging networking between senior leaders and high potential women, and including more women on shortlists. The roundtable lunches with senior leaders focus on their personal leadership journey. This is seen as an informal method of coaching that fulfils a dual purpose: on the one hand high potential women get exposure to senior leaders, which can increase their visibility; on the other hand senior leaders are invited to develop an awareness for central issues that women in the region might face. Including women on shortlists is an increasingly popular way to ensure that decision makers within the organization consider women. This does not mean that a quota for women in the organization is introduced. Instead it means that slates of candidates are gender diverse. The decision-making process is structured based on merit, yet women create visibility and hiring decisions that break the mould are encouraged. Although GE in MENAT recognizes that these changes are not made overnight, giving high potential women exposure to senior leaders and using diverse lists of candidates for appointment decisions can ensure that high potential women in the MENAT region can make a contribution to innovation. GE's leadership team realizes that there is an enormous amount of work to be done, but there is a strong commitment to invest in growing the next generation of leaders in MENAT in a gender-inclusive way.

Visibility means that one stands out. Women often stand out due to the fact that they are in a minority and thus unusual sights. This extra visibility can be very helpful when because senior leaders and clients might remember women. It also means that women can shine through top performance. However, mistakes are also more visible. This means that women will have to get it right. If they do not, their visibility can easily led to them being seen as failures rather than allowing them to learn through mistakes. In addition, the token woman becomes a representative of the category women, and making mistakes will be regarded as all women making these mistakes. Visibility for women means that they lose the ability to make and learn from mistakes in a safe environment. While high-risk projects provide Millennial women with the visibility needed to seen as a potential leader, it might be worthwhile considering ensuring that women do not shoulder disproportionately high risk. The organization also needs to work hard to ensure that Millennial women gain the ability to learn through their mistakes, which means that organizations need to develop mechanisms through which potential failures are constructed as learning experiences rather than failures of women as a group. This in turn can be achieved by strengthening psychological safety and ensuring that people in organizations feel safe to voice their opinion and to learn through mistakes.

Finally, on the pitfalls of appearance. The research has indicated how professional attire is largely in the eyes of the beholder, and that Millennial men and women still seem to find parameters of how to dress. Organizations should be very cautious to define only one style as the right dress style for them. For Millennials, authenticity will emerge through creating their own ways of dressing. Organizations should therefore embrace dress as a way by which individuals can express their individuality, but this obviously has boundaries, which are typically described in organizational policies. More importantly, it is crucial to allow women to express the degree of femininity and masculinity with which they are comfortable (that applies to men as well). Some guidance on what this means for the individual might be welcome, but restrictive statements, for instance about the authority-excerting abilities of certain pieces of attire, should be avoided. Millennials have the ability to figure out what they feel most comfortable with and some playful engagement with this will help them define their own professional style.

CONCLUSION

In this chapter we explored visibility, which is often seen as a central ingredient for leadership development. Networking in turn is key to developing visibility. As women are said to need more networking, women's networks are the obvious solution for developing women as leaders. However, many Millennial women are resistant to women's networks and do not feel at home there. They eschew simple one-cause explanations of their experience and at the same time lack a gender consciousness with which to analyse their experiences. It has therefore been suggested to ensure that networks work best if they are open to all and include men who are central change agents for changing organizations. Gender-balanced networks that are structured around generations can provide a fertile ground for discussing experience and introducing gender-conscious thinking to men and women. It is normally difficult to achieve visibility, but this applies mainly to men who need to stand out. For women standing out in male-dominated environments is fairly straightforward because they are often all-too-easily visible. This means that women miss out on the opportunity to learn through mistakes because their mistakes will not only be more visible but also their individual failure will be a collective failure for women. Organizations need to create safe environments for Millennial women to learn through mistakes. While the dress code for men in organizations is fairly straightforward, finding the right appearance requires work from women. Organizations can encourage women to find their own style and provide support, feedback and non-directive advice, but should shy away from providing a template for how women at work should look. The same is true for men, who would profit from some more latitude in their dress, which was something that Millennial men regularly talked about. Managing visibility is going to be central to developing Millennial leaders.

10

ORGANIZATIONAL CULTURE — THE POWER OF THE IDEAL WORKER

Nikhil came home late again. The current project he is working on means that he rarely comes home before 9 p.m. and has to be at work at 8 a.m. the next day. Weekends are filled with report writing and answering his backlog of emails for which he has not found time during the week. At least he can do this from home. With his daily commute this leaves little time for a private life and he has not seen the gym or met friends for months. Not surprisingly his diet leaves much to be desired. He never has breakfast and just picks up an extra-strong coffee and a chocolate bar in the morning. For lunch he normally buys some sandwiches, and the two-minute walk to the sandwich place is the only time he sees daylight, particularly now during the dark winter months. He eats the sandwich at his desk while trying to connect with his friends online, but he notices that fewer and fewer people respond to him. Maybe they are just busy but maybe they are annoyed because he has had to cancel too many appointments with them. Nikhil only leaves the office after his manager, who works very long hours, has left. That is what his manager expects from Nikhil as well. After all, the manager might need Nikhil to help and Nikhil enjoys being needed. After some caffeine and sweet snacks in the afternoon and early evening, he is usually too tired to prepare food. He sometimes picks up a ready-cooked meal on the way home or just warms up a frozen pizza. When he moved to London from India he had little idea that his life would be like this. The first time was great because he enjoyed being in London and meeting many new people. However when he started on his current project his work hours became extreme. He suffered from no longer having time for his social contacts and he felt that he had no life outside work.

Nikhil decided he needed a holiday. Since he had not seen his family for more than nine months, he decided to travel to India. His family commented on how thin and nervous he had become. He was irritable and could not eat properly after surviving all that time on fast food. Even on holiday he worked on the project by answering emails and sending back and forth spreadsheets that his boss had asked him to work on. His family grew increasingly concerned because he had problems waking up in the morning and worked through half the night. Nikhil was exhausted and decided to look for remedies for his various conditions. This is how he ended up going to a local ashram, where he learned to meditate and practise yoga under the guidance of a guru. He enjoyed the silence of the ashram and decided to stay there instead of going home. This meant that he had to surrender his beloved BlackBerry and his laptop, which were seen as distractions in the ashram. He spent just over a week in the ashram, which meant getting up early to practise meditation and yoga, to study ancient texts, listen to lectures and eating healthy. After leaving the ashram he felt rejuvenated and realized that he had to change his life.

Upon returning to London, he summoned the courage to make an appointment with his manager's boss, Robert. Jumping hierarchies did not come naturally to him, but he felt there was little point in talking to his line manager about his situation. His boss's boss agreed to meet him for a quick chat. Nikhil said that he loved working for the company and he sees potential for growth, but his current working hours were untenable and he wanted to have a life outside work. Robert was surprised to hear that Nikhil suffered from a lack of work–life balance because after all he presumed the company culture to be very supportive of such things. Robert explained that the organization is oriented towards end results rather than working time, which means that as long as Nikhil delivers his targets there is no need to be in the office all the time. Robert suggested having a conversation with Nikhil's manager about his workload and the sense of presenteeism that he imposed on Nikhil and other team members. During this conversation Nikhil's manager was surprised to learn that some team members felt that they had to stay until he leaves and that he expected emails to be answered immediately. He never said such things. But then again he did not explicitly state that people can leave before him or that he just sends emails whenever he has time but normally would not expect an answer in the evening or during weekends. The manager had a clarifying conversation with his team in which he spelled out what he expected and did not expect from them. Nikhil then felt that he had permission to not be in the office all the time, and developed a new routine which included fewer hours spent in the office, a healthy eating plan and time for exercise. There were still stressful times but Nikhil made an effort to stick to his routines and never felt as worn out as before.

In this chapter, we will take a look at the culture of organizations. We will break down what organizational cultures mean and how they are relevant for Millennial men and women. This will involve two elements: on the one hand, we will explore issues that are often called work–life balance; on the other hand we will highlight the assumptions and stereotypes that shape behaviour in the workplace. This chapter will be important to bring together some of the issues previously discussed and to specify ways to challenge and change them.

CULTURES OF ORGANIZATIONS – THE UNSPOKEN RULES AND THE IDEAL WORKER

Waiting in a comfortable reception area to be picked up by the person one is supposed to meet is regarded by many people as a waste of time. They eagerly check for new emails to make most of the time available. However, sitting in reception areas can be absolutely fascinating because it can tell you a lot about the organization. Observing how people interact, what they wear, or how slow or fast they walk gives you a glimpse into what binds individuals in the organization together to form a community. Visiting workspaces or going into a canteen has the same effect. What one gets a sense for is what makes this workplace tick. It gives you an insight into the organizational culture.

We regularly use the term 'organizational culture', but what we mean by it is often not clear. In fact, it is a bit of a catch-all term to describe things that we cannot quite put our finger on. Culture can be seen as the shared values, norms and assumptions that bind groups of people together. Culture helps us to explain how groups of people function together in an organization. Any stable group that shares a history will have its own culture, and in organizations culture is one of the key cornerstones that helps us to understand seemingly contradictory and irrational behaviour (Schein, 2010). Shared assumptions lead to shared 'rules'. Rules in this sense are not written down in a formal rulebook (although sometimes they are). Instead I am using rules in the anthropological sense, where rules can be compared to an unofficial code of conduct. They shape how people act and behave, but people are rarely conscious of the rules that they follow. They just do what they have learned is acceptable behaviour. Being initialized into an organizational culture normally happens during organizational socialization (Trice & Beyer, 1984). Once people are socialized into an organizational culture they understand the unspoken rules that guide behaviour in the organization.

Most work cultures are still shaped around what is called the protestant work ethic. This is a concept developed by sociologist Max Weber (Weber, 1934/1993) and refers to a situation in which an individual through his or her hard work earns salvation. This is a formulation of delayed gratification: by working hard now and delaying consumption and enjoyment, individuals earn their place in heaven. This work ethic means that it is one's duty to work hard. Self-control and hard work are not only rewarded with delayed gratification but also with the accumulation of capital, which is not used for consumption but is saved. Although the name protestant work ethic suggests a link to religion, which was certainly important in Weber's original work, the ideal worker is still working hard but often to enjoy immediate gratification. Working extreme jobs is seen as a badge of honour (Hewlett et al., 2007). However, in most secular Western societies delayed consumption is replaced by a hedonistic culture in which the rewards from working hard are enjoyed immediately through the acquisition of status-rich branded products.

This points to the fact that many individuals define themselves through work. Who they are depends on what type of work they are doing and how hard they work on it. The identity-forming parts of work were always more applicable to men than women. This is the case because women often form their identity through their private life (Wajcman, 1998). If people define themselves through their work, this gives meaning to their lives and shapes their identities. Working hard and foregoing a private life means constructing a certain identity that is modelled on the ideal worker. The ideal worker is the image in our mind of how the perfect employee looks in a respective organization. The ideal worker is constantly available for work and has no responsibilities outside work (Acker, 1990). Individuals who fit this template are promoted in organizations.

The ideal worker usually resides in the subconscious mind, and in that sense the ideal worker is a stereotype. In order to understand stereotypes it is helpful to explore what function they fulfil. We are exposed to a lot of information over the day and our mind simplifies this information for us by building categories. Rather than assessing every element of every incident anew, our mind builds categories for us, which means that we do not have to go through the process of assessing and evaluating every detail. These categories lead to stereotypes, which are simplified conceptions based on our own prior assumptions. Stereotypes need to be distinguished from prejudice. Prejudice is a negative emotional response to prior assumptions, whereas stereotypes do not necessarily contain an emotional response and they can be positive and negative.

The power of stereotypes is unfolded by the stereotype threat (Roberson & Kulik, 2007). A stereotype threat can impact any group for which a stereotype exists. A great example for this can be found in negotiation processes. While it is often assumed that women are less good negotiators than men, this is not substantiated by research except when they are negotiating for their own salary (Kray, Thompson & Galinsky, 2001). If women negotiate for themselves they confront stereotypes from their male and female counterparts. In light of this stereotype threat, women might shy away from negotiating their salaries. The good news is that stereotypes can be modified through what is called stereotype reactance (Roberson & Kulik, 2007). Stereotypes are often compared to an iceberg, where only the tip of the iceberg is visible but the majority of the iceberg is under water. The model is often attributed to Sigmund Freud, who is said to have used the iceberg metaphor to describe the difference between the conscious and unconscious mind (Westen, 1999). Stereotype reactance tells us that by making stereotypes visible, we become conscious of them and can react to and subvert them. This means that instead of being aware only of the tip of the iceberg, we realize its fuller dimensions. Without being aware of stereotypes in the unconscious, it is difficult to react to them. For our negotiation example, this means the following. If women draw attention to the fact that they are women by, for instance, pointing out that they are the main breadwinner, this means that stereotypes move to the conscious level. Experiments have shown that in those cases where gender stereotypes are flagged up, differences in negotiation success disappear.

As a stereotype the ideal worker often shapes our expectations of work unconsciously. It also shapes the working practices people engage in at work and the overall culture of the organization. The ideal worker will be influential in including those who comply with the norms of the ideal worker; those who do not will be excluded. The success and failure of any initiatives to develop alternative approaches to work–life integration and to reshape the organizational culture will depend on their ability to make the stereotypes surrounding the ideal worker visible and increase consciousness of them. This will allow change to happen.

BEYOND BALANCE – WORK–LIFE INTEGRATION

It is first useful to define some of the terms that are used in the arena of work–life balance. Work–life balance is commonly used to mean a situation where work and life outside work are in equilibrium. How this equilibrium looks on an individual basis is highly personal and it rarely ever means an equal time spent on work and life outside work. Life outside work can in itself mean different things. It can mean family and friends, it can mean doing household chores, it can mean pursing a hobby (Özbilgin et al., 2011). If work and life are perceived as out of balance this means that stress is produced. The notion of balance suggests some kind of equilibrium, but how this equilibrium is defined is highly individual. I find the term 'work–life balance' misleading and prefer to talk about work–life integration and the work–life nexus. Work–life integration means that paid employment and a life outside work are integrated in a unique combination (Kossek & Lambert, 2005). Work–life nexus refers to the interface between work and life.

Work–life integration is often linked to a range of flexible work practices, which allow individuals to integrate work and life. Flexible working practices can include time and space. Time refers to different forms of non-standard work hours, which means the departure of the regular full-time working time defined in any given country, and can include flexible start and end times of work, condensed hours in the week or the year, and so on. In regard to space, this means that work no longer has to be done in the office but can be done at any location they employee chooses, such as their home or a café. The physical office environment remains an important hub for communication and the exchange of ideas. This is often called an extensification of work because work is no longer only happening in the office (Jarvis & Pratt, 2006). In organizations this is often called agile working. Most approaches to flexible working have tried to reshape an industrial workspace in which work processes were different, but agile working seems to go further in allowing a reimagination of how work in the twenty-first century will look in regard to space and time.

Research has shown that while work–life integration initiatives are often constructed as though they are for everyone, they tend to be taken up by women (Smithson & Stokoe, 2005). Many organizations believe that women's different life cycles need to be considered and that this will help women to advance. In general this means catering for women's potential motherhood and ensuring that they are not disadvantaged in their careers due to having children. Flexible working and having a life outside work is in many organizations still a stigma in spite of the many policies that seem to postulate that working flexibly is wanted. In Britain 45% of women work in part-time arrangements, and most women work in part-time arrangements at one point in their lives (Manning & Petrongolo, 2008). This has major implications for pay which is called the 'part-time penalty'. Women working part-time in the UK earn 25% less than those working full-time, and this differential has increased in the last 30 years (Manning & Petrongolo, 2008).

Working a flexible schedule also often means that training is neglected and promotional opportunities disappear. Asking for flexible working arrangements is for many women seen as risky because they might be perceived as being not career-minded and are therefore not interested in advancing their career (Liff & Ward, 2001). An Employee Relations Survey which comprised 28,240 respondents in the UK, has indeed shown that women on non-standard contracts are less likely to have discussed promotional opportunities and training needs (Hoque & Kirkpatrick, 2003). They also received less training. This was not the case for men on non-standard employment contracts. It is thereby suggested that women working in flexible arrangements are more likely to lose out on training and career development.

Although work–life integration is regularly discussed in relation to women in the workplace and particularly working mothers, for Millennials having a life outside work is important, too. Cross-temporal meta-analyses have shown that Millennials place more value on leisure than previous generations (Twenge et al., 2010). This is linked to the wish for work–life integration that Millennials often voice. For most Millennials this means having a life outside work which will contain travelling, meeting friends and pursuing hobbies. Having literally grown up with technology means that Millennials understand that work no longer has to be done from an office in a rigid 9–5 framework. Although research evidence on the working practices that Millennials prefer in regard to work–life integration is still scarce, it shows that work–life integration is no longer an issue for working mothers only. A much wider part of the working population will demand work–life integration through the potential that technologies offer.

In sum, it can be argued that workplaces have to be re-invented to move working practices truly into the twenty-first century. However, approaches to work–life integration were centred mainly on one group of the workplace, working mothers, who by working flexibly would often forgo training and career development. Working mothers, however, are no longer the only group that demands work–life integration: Millennials value leisure time and this makes them more likely to value work–life integration. However, the lack of work–life integration in current workplaces goes beyond a focus on working practices but instead urges us to look at the model that is underlying work as we understand it.

THE LONG-HOURS CULTURE

In our interviews with the Millennials, one of the issues around work–life integration that came up regularly related to experiences with the long-hours culture. In our sample, we found a variety of attitudes that Millennials displayed in relation to work–life integration. Some worked very long hours to advance their careers, others tolerated long hours only temporarily. Some Millennials also voiced their frustration with the long-hours culture. Regardless of their different views on long hours, having a choice about working long hours was seen by all Millennials as important.

Some people indicated that they worked all hours available to progress in their career. These were the driven individuals who see that the only way to progress in the organization is through working long hours. Juan provides a good example of this. Juan is originally from Brazil and has been working in the UK for four years. He said that he does not mind working long hours. He is single and likes to work hard. He attributed his attitude to the fact that he is Brazilian and in Brazil in his view people work long hours. Fourteen-hour days are therefore not a problem for him, but his colleagues always complain about this and want to leave the organization due to the hours. For him, he likes to work hard. However, he acknowledges that this might change once he is married and has a family, when he expects to work less.

Stefan also talked about he long hours he worked. He says that he enjoys work and does not mind working long hours, but he also states that he misses his wife while at work and that once he has children he will need to ensure that he makes more time for the family. I found Stefan's work arrangements chilling. He described how he worked very long hours and left work at around 9 p.m. to commute home, which took him about two hours. He would then work for three or four hours at home, normally going to bed around 2 a.m. only to wake at 6:30 a.m. to be at work at 9 a.m. His expectation of the weekend was to 'only' work for eight hours a day. In his view, he had to put the hours in to progress. I asked him if his manager knew about his night shifts and Stefan denied that. He did not want to mention that he worked an additional three to four hours a night and full day shifts on weekends because he would then look as though he was unable to finish his work in the normal working time. In order for him to progress in the organization, he felt that he had to work the extra hours.

Imelda also worked in excess of 60 hours a week, but she described her current job as less time-consuming than her previous job, for which she worked more than 75 hours a week. She also states that she attempts to take weekends off but works on average four hours every other Sunday. Imelda is focused on her career and she expects that her long hours will translate into a higher salary in the run long. She states that her current life arrangements allow her to work long hours. Her partner, who is employed in a consultancy, works equally long hours and travels a lot. Imelda is also thinking about how this arrangement might change once they have children. Her life plans include her partner by then being senior enough in the consultancy where he works to have a more flexible schedule and less travelling. She expects him to take a bigger role in bringing up the children, which will allow her to advance her career further.

For most people, however, working long hours was mainly a question of being in a stressful period in a project. Vernon, for instance, talked about how his organization required flexibility from him to work long hours and that this was a normal part of doing business. He acknowledged that he would cut back on sleep and social contacts to fulfil the project requirements but he would not do this all the time. Ian similarly said that sometimes long hours are required in order to finish a project and that this arrangement is fine for him as long as it is temporary and he is rewarded for it. Kareena also said that it is reasonable to expect long hours as long as one is given a break afterwards. Sven similarly presumed that he would work long hours for a limited period of time but not longer than six months because of the strain this puts on relationships not only with his girlfriend but also with friends generally.

There were also Millennials that were sceptical about the lack of time that existed for their private activities. Christine said that in the UK life seems to evolve around the office and one has little time to prepare and eat food or spend time with one's family. She even finds it difficult to phone her family due to the time pressures at work. She also described the long-hours culture as a social epidemic that is particularly prevalent in people-centred businesses where organizations are trying to squeeze out as much labour as they can. She is very much aware that she does not want to wake up one day to wonder where her life has gone. Christine dreams about setting up her own company because then at least she would know that she can earn the rewards of 18-hour days, whereas in her current job she does not see much benefit from signing her life away. For Christine owning her own business would also help her to set her own hours, which she perceived as more conducive to having and caring for a family.

Paula similarly talked about how she is prepared to work long hours but does not think that they are sustainable. She thinks it is important to have the time to be with family and friends. For her to achieve this sustainability she sets herself clear boundaries, such as on what time she leaves the office. Uma also talked about how being on client sites left a mark on her private life and health. Being away Monday to Thursday meant that she did not see her partner much and it also meant that she was not eating very healthily. This arrangement made her physically sick and she described how happy she was to complete the project. Olivia made similar comments about how travelling made her so tired that she went straight to bed once she got home and slept through the weekend.

While there was a great variety of perspectives on the long-hours culture, it was noticeable that Millennials shared a common perspective: they wanted the choice to set their own working times. Stefan describes it as his own choice to work long hours to advance his career. Similarly, Imelda talked about that working long hours was down to her own decision making rather than external requests. Kareena also stated that long hours are okay temporarily, as long as she gets the autonomy to make up for the intense period of work later on. Paula made the choice to set herself boundaries to avoid being sucked into the long-hours culture.

The notion of choice is a complex one in social research because much of what people might perceive as choice is in fact not a choice at all but a requirement to live in a society or to succeed in an organization. In order words, in order to advance in an organization prioritizing professional life over private life and working long hours might be a requirement of the ideal worker. Those who comply with this ideal will advance; those who do not are likely to be left behind. What we see in relation to the long-hours culture is that there is still the unspoken rule in organizations that the ideal worker will work long hours. The norms that transpire through these accounts are that long hours are expected when needed. The ideal worker still has to be available at all hours in order to fulfil the requirements of deadlines at work. Millennials are aware of those norms and they accept them. They also want to receive some kind of reward for working long hours, which can include time off, a financial reward or a promotion. Most Millennials constructed working long hours and sacrificing their private life as a choice for them that they made consciously. This provides Millennials with the illusion of being in control of their own work–life choices, whereas instead they seem to be dictated by the ideal worker norm.

BELONGING IN TRANSIENT WORKING PRACTICES

While Millennials are often thought to embrace flexible working practices, what we regularly heard were examples of feeling simultaneously empowered and isolated through working practices that encouraged flexible working. Although Millennials, as digital natives, are used to working flexibly, they missed a community at work. This expressed itself in relation to friends and community activities like volunteering.

Christine participated in one of the induction programmes that are common for new graduates in many organizations. She particularly commented on the fact that she met many people who became her friends. She cites those friends as an important peer group that helps her better understand the organizational culture and appropriate ways of behaviour. This was echoed by others who regularly stressed that friendship at work was important to them. Kareena, for instance, talked about how important it is for her to have friends at work rather than just workmates. This improves the work climate for her and means that it feels for her like she is coming to work to spend time with friends. Maya also commented on the fact that many people she met in her workplace will be her friends for life. We thereby see how work relationships are transformed into friendships that extend beyond the workplace. This illustrates that for many Millennials the friendships that they develop in the workplace are crucial for them.

These friendships are even more important in a world of work where flexibility in regards to time and space is becoming the norm. Christine talked about the fact that she enjoys mobile working, which means working in chic and flexible offices where everything is done electronically. She also loves the flexibility of working different hours and travelling. She also talked about the feeling that her laptop becomes another appendage for her, almost becoming part of herself. Technology is becoming an extension of herself. However, she acknowledges that there is a downside to this, which is the fact that she never has any stability. She is always on the move instead of having a normal 9–5 office job. Her job never ends, which is a problem for making space for creative thinking. She likens this experience to writing essays at university: instead of writing the essay there is always something else to do that needs her immediate attention. What she talks about is a lack of routine and a lack of time for reflection, which is sidelined in a dynamic work environment where immediacy is key.

This feeling of being 'uprooted' was echoed by others, such as Tina. She talked about how difficult she finds it to move from project to project, always with new people and always very tight deliverables. She experienced an intense camaraderie during the projects but those intense bonds are broken up quickly when she moves on to the next project and the old team is forgotten. This transient existence of working together in teams which are then broken up contributes to people's struggle to develop a stable identity over time (Sennett, 1998). At the same time Tina enjoys the mobility of her job. Kareena also talked about how no one had time to explain anything to her but she was expected to fix certain things in the project. For her this was exciting due to the responsibility she received, but also daunting because she was not sure that she was doing the right thing. Yet at the same time this allowed her to learn on the job.

Many Millennials also talked about the isolation they experience on a daily basis. Stefan, for instance talked about how strange it was to come into the open plan office every day and just sit down and start to work. He does not say 'hello' and 'good morning' to the person next to him because in many cases he is unable to sit with his team. Tessa talked about how difficult she found it to deal with people over the phone and email rather than walking over to them to ask them directly. Another drawback of flexible working was voiced by April. When she first joined she had no idea where to sit and how to find the canteen. April described that luckily she met a woman who showed her around, but she remembers the feeling of being lost dominating her first days at work. April said that she started to develop her own community based on the graduate cohort with which she started. Even though they were working on different projects, they decided to sit together to have shared space and people to talk to. Similarly, William, who had a prior career in the military service, talked about the lack of camaraderie that he encountered in the organization. Many Millennials talked about the fact that in many cases there was a lot of competition among peer groups and in the organization overall. While people might develop bonds, it was also clear that they were ultimately competing for the interesting projects and the promotions. While teams might hold together for a short period of time, the organization as a whole felt a bit disparate to many Millennials and thus lacked a feeling of belonging.

One way in which belonging was created was through volunteering and 'giving back'. Most Millennials told us that monetary rewards as well as personal development were central to their choice to join the organization. The much-cited wish for Millennials to have organizations that are strong in corporate responsibility was more of a bonus rather than the ultimate element on which decisions to join a company were based. While corporate responsibility was not a necessary condition, many Millennials talked about how they enjoyed participating in volunteering activities. Charlie, for instance, mentioned how he enjoyed giving back by representing the company at universities or by participating in charity football matches. Uma said that she had recently applied to participate in a competition that involves working a project that improves the world. Although she is not sure what to expect she is grateful that the company allows her to participate and gives her time off for doing so. Those times to volunteer allow Millennials to bond with other people and to feel as though they are giving back to the community. These volunteering opportunities allow Millennials to develop bonds with others and to improve their self-worth.

For the junior professionals we interviewed starting with the organizations meant that they were joining companies where flexible working was practised. Given the fact that Millennials are described as digital natives one might assume that the flexible working practices they encountered in organizations was what they expected work to be like. Even though the Millennials had grown up as technologies that allow flexible working were maturing, the Millennials experienced flexible working as simultaneously empowering and uprooting. When starting in a new organization they wanted to plant their roots and develop a strong community at work. In many cases, they wanted their work colleagues to be their friends. However many Millennials felt isolated at work, which led to the sense that they did not have an immediate community. Apart from their peer group and the bonds that developed in teams many Millennials also received a sense of community through their volunteering work. It thereby appears that in times of flexible working, creating a sense of belonging through friendship and community work are central.

MEANING-GIVING PRACTICES

Although work–life integration is often seen as an issue for women, work–life integration was at the top of the agenda for Millennials. Many men and women were happy to work long hours but they were aware that they wanted to have time for themselves either now or in the future when they would have families. Yet what Millennials encountered is an ideal worker who is constantly available for work and can work all hours required. The culture in their organizations dictates this availability. Although Millennials like working flexibly, many Millennials felt isolated from their peer group and their teams and struggled to develop a sense of community. This was often done through volunteer work. They also felt that the pressures of project work allowed little opportunity to focus on tasks that required more time and concentration.

What many Millennials experience is a lack of routine. Millennials in our interviews were quick to point out that routines were often associated with boredom and not advancing anymore. However, at the same time it was staggeringly clear that what many Millennials lacked in the organizational cultures were routines that allowed them to introduce some stability into their working lives. The constant transient way of existing left them feeling uprooted. Routines are a useful way of developing those roots and the stability they craved. Routines embody those grounding structures that are needed by many Millennials. However, routines not only stabilize and reproduce; they can also be the mechanism for change (Feldman & Pentland, 2003). Routines thus not only reproduce the status quo, they might also introduce subtle change over time.

Concretely this means that for Millennials routines can provide structure. An example is allowing one or two hours a day to work on reports and similar writing projects. Routines can also mean planning certain times when emails are responded to and scheduling regular lunch meetings with colleagues and friends. These routines also mean having a stable working time and setting clear boundaries to avoid life being consumed by work. They also mean organizing daily activities in those areas that give Millennials energy and those that they perceive as draining. This will allow them to ensure that they have enough energy-giving activities in a day and in a week to balance the energy-draining activities. This has to be embedded in routines. Such routines permit the boundary setting that many Millennials need to avoid burning out.

Other meaning-giving practices should centre around community. Workspaces in which Millennials flourish need to be designed in such a way as to allow people to collaborate and socialize. Many organizations led the way by creating workspaces in which individuals not only sit at their desks but also share meals, find contemplation and work with others. It is not surprising that in recent years many organizational spaces were transformed into public living rooms where individuals congregate. Those spaces will allow communities to be formed. In addition to space, providing employees with time to give back will remain important. While Millennials are not more altruistic than previous generations, volunteering and similar activities of giving back can help create a community spirit that provides Millennials with meaning.

While Millennials provide one pressure point for organizations to change, the organizational culture needs to be altered more substantially to allow the template of the ideal worker to be widened. In many routine interactions gender patterns are embedded and lead through assumptions and stereotypes to subtle discrimination. Many mid-level and senior managers do not consciously discriminate against everyone who does not fulfil the ideal worker standards. But the embeddedness of stereotypes in these routines lead to the fact that exclusion is reproduced. One way of becoming aware of such discriminatory routines is to move these routines from an unconscious to a conscious level. Many organizations use unconscious bias training for this purpose. While these one-off initiatives are helpful in communicating the 'bigger picture', it is vitally important to break the routines in daily life. This means that mid-level managers and senior leaders need to reflect every day on how actions in the organization might be gendered. This does not have to be for a long period of time; it can literally be a couple of minutes each day. This will allow managers to become conscious of some of the routines that are limiting the success of non-ideal workers.

SIGNATURE PRACTICE: CHANGING ORGANIZATIONAL CULTURES

Many organizations have realized that it is the organizational culture that limits meritocracy. A common answer to this is bias awareness or unconscious bias training which is very often delivered to the top management team. However, often the challenge is how the theoretical insight that people have biases can be translated into everyday work situations. In everyday work situations people have less time to think about their actions and it is there that bias can unfold its power.

This is why PwC's UK practice has taken bias awareness training a step further. Based on a recommendation from the board, PwC started to develop bias awareness training for all employees and unusually made it mandatory. This was the first time that such an approach was adopted for non-regulatory training at PwC. This indicates how important the firm saw it to raise awareness for how inclusionary behaviour can be facilitated. The training was delivered via an e-learning offering which was framed in a positive way by talking about open minds rather than biases.[1] It also addressed different learning style through using media such as videos, recorded talks, psychological testing and email prompts.

The email prompts were an innovative approach to take the content of the bias awareness training programme outside of a formalized learning approach into the everyday life of employees. People would receive an email prompt asking them to reflect on their behaviour. An employee might be encouraged to reflect on any situation during a particular day where he or she judged someone else based on bias. This is important because all too often the theoretical insight that people have biases gets lost in real-life situations where decisions have to be made quickly. It is there that our minds revert to stereotypes and biases because it saves times and makes responses quicker. Bringing the bias awareness training into real-job situations encourages people to reflect and potentially avoid similar biases in the future.

Almost all of the 16,000 employees of PwC UK have completed the training in the required time. All new joiners are required to take the training. The impacts of the campaign express themselves in the fact that employees are given a new vocabulary to think and act in inclusive ways. The initiative also won an Opportunity Now Award (Opportunity Now, 2012). The innovative part of the training was to move it from the stage of theoretical insight in a training situation to everyday situations. It underscores the commitment PwC is making towards creating an organizational culture that is inclusive. In such a culture Millennials, women and particularly Millennial women will thrive.

This means that in order to break the ideal worker template, organizations have to become more inclusive. Although many Millennials describe their ability and willingness to work long hours as a matter of choice, this choice is curtailed by who can be an ideal worker. As long as the overarching template of the ideal worker is seen as working long hours, it is unlikely that Millennials alone will be able to change the template. In order to achieve inclusion, the culture of organizations needs to change in the number of variations they allow the ideal worker. Work–life integration is one example of this, but a true understanding of how inclusion can be achieved and the template of the ideal worker can be widened goes much beyond that. It requires senior leaders and mid-level managers to appreciate the importance of gender, diversity and inclusion to change the overall culture of organizations.

CONCLUSION

In this chapter we have looked at organizational cultures from the perspective of the ideal worker. The ideal worker is always available for work and has no life outside work. This ideal worker model is said to restrict women progressing in organizations, but it also restricts others who do not fulfil the ideal worker template. Although many work–life integration programmes are designed with women at their heart, research evidence has shown that for Millennials work–life integration is important and that Millennials can be motivated to stay with an employer if they can enjoy their leisure time and are granted sabbaticals for travel and the like. While there are different perspectives on the long-hours culture, it became evident that many Millennials understood working long hours as a choice. However, this choice was framed by the ability and wish to be an ideal worker for whom working long hours is the norm, at least during this stage of their lives. Millennials also felt that transient working practices were empowering and isolating at the same time. Organizations are therefore encouraged to build communities in the workplace in providing spaces to socialize with friends and colleagues and in encourage employees to be active in the community. In addition, creating grounding rituals in daily practices can help Millennials experience more grounding and stability. This will provide Millennials with a sense of belonging and meaning. However, Millennials cannot change the ideal worker template on their own. Senior leaders and mid-level managers need to understand how the ideal worker template can be broadened and how often their own decisions are clouded by biases and perceptions. Changing the ideal worker template is an effort for the entire organization and has to go beyond a focus on work–life practices and focus on a wider range of practices to create inclusion. For today's managers and leaders it is important to become aware of the stereotypes they might hold. If today's managers and leaders are made aware of the limiting effects of some of those stereotypes and biases, they are able to reshape them in such a way as to allow diverse people to be included in the workplace and inclusive leaders to rise to the top of organizations.

11

CONCLUSION

INTRODUCTION

At the beginning of the book we met Leonora, who decided to figure out what she wanted from work and life by consulting a career coach. Although she had had a stellar career so far, she felt that in recent times her aims, goals and ambitions had come under scrutiny. In the opening chapter we looked through Leonora's eyes to understand some of her thought processes. The themes with which Leonora was concerned are all reflected in the heuristic we developed in this book. Discussing Leonora's experience through the heuristic will allow us to understand better what the heuristic means in practice.

Leonora did not really find any *role models* in her environment that she thought were perfect and that she wanted to emulate. While there were some impressive women, there was always something that was not right with the senior women. For Leonora it might be useful to think about building a composite role model of all the abilities, skills and behaviours that her role model should have without emulating one person. Leonora should grow confident enough to admire a role model without idealizing them. Leonora's career would also profit from her earning the sponsorship of a senior man or woman who could help advance her career. Leonora also felt that she could not be herself at work, which she experienced as draining. She has to learn that authentic leadership does not mean being oneself at work but displaying a behaviour that is perceived by others as appropriate and professional. Leonora should also find an organization that does not try to clone its leaders but one that is keen to promote leaders who break the mould. She should also start to think about how she can tell her own life story in such a way that others can relate to it.

Leonora is keen to learn and feedback is central for her to keep learning. This wish for *experiential learning* is very common for Millennials, who understand that learning through feedback will allow them to be better at their job and to ensure their employability. She should therefore seek as much feedback as possible from her peers and superiors. This will ensure that she learns through experience. In regard to *formal education*, Leonora was thinking about embarking on an MBA degree but was concerned about some of the experiences her friends reported on in regard to the masculine culture of business schools. Leonora would be well advised to seek out the cultures of potential MBA schools and select one where she feels that she can grow and develop her skills. A business schools that focuses on developing inclusive leaders through education inside and outside the classroom might be a good choice for her.

Leonora will have to develop her *visibility* in order to advance in the organization. She was very closely associated with a project that failed, and she feels that being associated with this project has tarnished her identity. Her visibility limits her ability to make mistakes. She would therefore be well advised to discuss assignments with her superior so that she can make mistakes in a safe environment. The *organizational culture* that Leonora confronts might appear unchangeable and set in stone. However, there are certain ways that she can manipulate stereotypes and biases, such as remembering that making those stereotypes visible is central to overcoming them. This will allow Leonora to work creatively with the culture she confronts and to make small gains.

Using the heuristic allows us to understand Leonora's experience better and suggest some possible ways of action. However, this is only part of the story. In many cases it is organizations that need to facilitate change in order to retain and develop rising stars like Leonora. In this final chapter, I will weave the different threads of this research together to allow a more connected perspective on how Millennial women can be developed as leaders.

FROM DEVELOPING THE HEURISTIC TO APPLYING IT

At the centre of this book was the question of how gender, generation and leadership interact. We explored this question by looking at how Millennial women can be developed into leaders. Generations were defined on three different definitions, which included the age-based, cohort-based and incumbency-based definitions. The focus of this book was Millennials, who are the latest entrants into organizations. Gender was defined as referring to both men and women and is understood from a constructivist rather than a biologistic perspective. The focus in this book was on women in relation to men. This was the basis for creating a heuristic for developing

Millennial women as leaders (Figure 11.1). It was also discussed how the book draws on empirical research and reactions to its communication to feed a double hermeneutic where theory influences practice and practice influences theory.

The second chapter focused on gender and leadership by first reviewing general issues for women in organizations and then offering a critical perspective on the business case for gender and diversity. I then highlighted different ways of framing gender change in organizations, ranging from making women more like men, through valuing gender difference, to finally widening the template. The framing used in this book is the last of these. The chapter continued to develop the six elements of the heuristic by exploring approaches to gender-sensitive leadership development. The third chapter explored the academic literature on Millennials to highlight trait changes from one generation to the next. The average Millennial can be characterized as confident, authentic, anxious

© *Elisabeth Kelan 2012*

Figure 11.1 The heuristic for developing Millennial women as leaders

(particularly in face of ambiguity), assertive, money-driven and leisure time loving. The quarter-life crisis and the changes in technology and the workplace were also discussed. The chapter cumulated in exploring what leadership development means from a generational perspective by adding an additional layer to the heuristic. The fourth chapter then developed the last stage of the heuristic by paying attention to research on Millennial men and women. We first traced changes in perceptions of gendered skills and the decline of the male breadwinner model before discussing Millennial women's views on feminism. These insights were then taken together for the final layer of the heuristic.

After developing the heuristic, the different dimensions were discussed based on the empirical evidence in the subsequent chapters. The first two chapters focused on self-knowledge, which included role models and authenticity. Role models were considered as forms of identification at work and were related to sponsors and mentors. The idealized, yet aggrandized role model for Millennials is the authentic, self-made CEO or founder. When female role models were talked about they tended to be admired rather than idealized, which means that their skills, attributes and behaviour were discussed more critically and only partially accepted. It was argued that this can be taken even further by encouraging Millennial women to develop composite role models through which they combine behaviours and traits from multiple persons. This is a model for both men and women. It was also discussed that junior and senior men should be paired in formal mentoring programmes with junior and senior women to raise awareness of potential gender issues in men and women.

Chapter 6 looked at authenticity. We defined this as self-awareness that needs to be recognized by others so that they perceive a leader as authentic. We also looked at authenticity as a narrative that can be used for leadership development. Authenticity also relates to the division between the public and private sphere, which was explored from a gender and generational perspective. It was stressed that for Millennials it is important to develop self-narratives that are perceived by others as authentic. For women this often means combining elements that can be read as masculine and feminine. This was also seen as a way for men to develop greater authenticity.

The next two chapters explored knowledge acquisition through experiential and formal education. Experiential learning relates to on-the-job-training which is gaining importance in a time of changing careers when feedback is important to ensure employability. This explains why it is so important for Millennials to receive feedback and to learn. The importance of feedback was linked to online interactions in social media, and coaching was seen as a way for Millennials to receive individualized advice. Millennials can be engaged in organizations through feedback and coaching.

These chapters were followed by a focus on formal education, which in this case was an MBA degree. At a time when careers are changing, formal education such as completing an MBA remains a rite of passage that indicates a transition in status from being a junior person in the organization to being someone more senior. It was shown that strong bonds and a strong sense of community are formed in this rite of passage. However, these strong communities also mean that difference is systematically ignored and silenced. Bringing gender to the fore was thereby seen as problematic because it threatened the community through the introduction of difference. It was shown that this not only limits the experience in business schools but will also lead to developing leaders that cannot manage inclusivity and who struggle to be effective coaches.

The final two substantial chapters concerned social knowledge through visibility and understanding the organizational culture. Visibility is a double-edged sword for women. Women are particularly scarce in senior positions and therefore stand out more. This also limits their ability to make mistakes and learn from them. The chapter was particularly concerned with networking and appearance. While women's networks have been seen as central for not only providing support but also visibility, Millennial women are often sceptical towards them. It was suggested that networks should include men as well as women, and sometimes it is beneficial not to focus too much on gender. Directives on appearance and dress were perceived by Millennial women as limiting their authenticity and it was also suggested that men would profit from more latitude in relation to dress. It is also important that organizations create environments where women can learn through mistakes. Managing visibility is central for developing Millennials into leaders.

The final chapter focused on organizational cultures. We focused on the ideal worker and the unspoken rules that determine organizational cultures. The ideal worker is always available for work and has no life outside work. Attitudes and behaviours towards work–life integration are influenced to a large degree by the organizational culture and the ideal worker conceptualization. For Millennials the long-hours culture in their organizations is seen as a choice, yet they have to comply with it in order to be seen as ideal workers. Millennials also felt that transient working practices were empowering and isolating at the same time. It was therefore suggested that organizations should create spaces where individuals can collaborate in an informal environment. Although Millennials dislike routines, they can help to provide grounding and stability. Changing the ideal worker is, however, a task for organizations and they need to break down the stereotypes and biases of their workforce in order to allow alternative ideal workers to gain prominence.

FROM THEORY TO PRACTICE AND BACK

The heuristic for developing Millennial women as leaders is way of thinking through some of the challenges and opportunities that the intersections between gender and generation bring to organizations. It highlights some of the areas of tension when thinking about developing junior women as leaders. In this book I have used evidence from empirical academic research to shed light on the gender and generation nexus. I also included examples that were collected through more informal research methods such as giving talks in organizations. This ensures that the research resonates with practice. The focus on practice was also helped by exploring specific signature practices that have been adopted by organizations. The insights gained from practice connected in many ways to the academic insights and in fact often provided additional angles and further grounds from which to advance the theoretical arguments.

This book does not claim to offer a 'recipe' for how to develop women as leaders but instead offers some areas for reflection. As outlined in the introduction, the practices portrayed in this book alongside the theoretical insights are not expected to form a restrictive template that organizations can follow in solving the issue of the scarcity of women leaders. It is not best practice that is just waiting to be emulated by organizations. Instead this book should be understood as highlighting theoretical insights and signature practices that can help stimulate thinking and discussions that might lead to new practices that facilitate change and that fit different organizations. This book should therefore be understood as a companion to spark this reflective process.

CONCLUSION

In this final chapter a summary of the book and its contribution in relation to theory and practice has been offered. The book has developed a heuristic with which to think through the development of Millennial women as leaders. The heuristic focused on six dimensions: role models, authenticity, experiential learning, formal education, visibility and organizational culture. In the first part of the book academic research evidence was used to explore what these dimensions mean form a perspective of gender, generations and gender/generations. This was followed by an in-depth exploration of the individual dimensions, drawing on my own research evidence in terms of academic interviews and corporate signature practices. This book should be understood as inspiring reflection on how to develop Millennial women as leaders that might spark initiatives and practices to achieve this goal. These initiatives and practices might ignite the potential of Millennial men and women to evolve into inclusive leaders who break the mould.

NOTES

1 INTRODUCTION

1   Social scientific research often uses 'race' to denote the social construction of race rather than presuming a biological basis. This is similar to the social construction of gender discussed in this chapter.

2 WOMEN AS LEADERS

1   There is however a disparity in what women study: women study health- and welfare-related subjects, and the humanities, arts and education; men prefer engineering, manufacturing and construction followed by mathematics and computer science. Equal numbers of men and women choose life sciences, physical sciences, agriculture, social sciences, business studies and law (OECD, 2012).

3 MILLENNIALS AS LEADERS

1   This is somewhat surprising given the fact that the construction of father-hood seems to have changed significantly over the last decades, with many fathers being actively involved in bringing up their children (Cooper, 2000). It is also interesting to note that much of the domestic work and care work is today performed by women (and increasingly men) from less developed regions of the world (Ehrenreich & Hochschild, 2003).

10 ORGANIZATIONAL CULTURE – THE POWER OF THE IDEAL WORKER

1   This reflects current research evidence on the positive framing of diversity and inclusion initiatives (Jayne & Dipboye, 2004).

REFERENCES

Acker, J. 1990. 'Hierarchies, Jobs, Bodies: A Theory of Gendered Organizations'. *Gender & Society*, 4(2): 139–58.

Adkins, L. 2000. 'Objects of Innovation: Post-Occupational Reflexivity and Re-Traditionalisation of Gender'. In S. Ahmed, J. Kilby, C. Lury, M. McNeil and B. Skeggs (eds), *Transformations: Thinking through Feminism*: 259–72. London: Routledge.

Allmendinger, J. 2009. *Frauen auf dem Sprung – Wie junge Frauen heute leben wollen – Die BRIGITTE-Studie*. München: Pantheon.

Allmendinger, J. and Hackman, J. R. 1995. 'The More, the Better? A Four-Nation Study of the Inclusion of Women in Symphony Orchestras'. *Social Forces*, 74(2): 423–60.

Arthur, C. 2011. 'Berners-Lee Says Jobs Made Computing "Usable Rather Than Infuriating"'. http://www.guardian.co.uk/technology/blog/2011/oct/16/tim-berners-lee-steve-jobs.

Arthur, M. B. 1994. 'The Boundaryless Career: A New Perspective for Organizational Enquiry'. *Journal of Organizational Behavior*, 15(4): 295–306.

Arthur, M. B. and Rousseau, D. M. 1996. 'Introduction: The Boundaryless Career as a New Employment Principle'. In M. B. Arthur and D. M. Rousseau (eds), *The Boundaryless Career – A New Employment Principle for a New Organizational Era*: 3–20. Oxford: Oxford University Press.

Atwood, J. D. and Scholtz, C. 2008. 'The Quarter-Life Time Period: An Age of Indulgence, Crisis or Both?' *Contemporary Family Therapy*, 30(4): 233–50.

Avolio, B. J. and Gardner, W. L. 2005. 'Authentic Leadership Development: Getting to the Root of Positive Forms of Leadership'. *The Leadership Quarterly*, 16(3): 315–38.

Banyard, K. 2011. *The Equality Illusion: The Truth about Women and Men Today*. London: Faber and Faber.

Baumgardner, J. and Richards, A. 2000. *Manifesta: Young Women, Feminism, and the Future*. New York: Farrar, Straus and Giroux.

Beauvoir, S. de. 1949/1993. *The Second Sex*. London: Everyman's Library.

Beck, U. 1992. *Risk Society: Towards a New Modernity*. London: Sage.

Beck, U. 2000. *The Brave New World of Work*. Cambridge: Polity.

Beck, U., Giddens, A. and Lash, S. 1994. *Reflexive Modernization – Politics, Tradition and Aesthetics in the Modern Social Order*. Cambridge: Polity Press.

REFERENCES

Bergman, S. M., Fearrington, M. E., Davenport, S. W. and Bergman, J. Z. 2011. 'Millennials, Narcissism, and Social Networking: What Narcissists do on Social Networking Sites and Why'. *Personality and Individual Differences*, 50(5): 706–11.

Bierema, L. L. 2005. 'Women's Networks: A Career Development Intervention or Impediment?' *Human Resource Development International*, 8(2): 207–24.

Blanchard, M. 1991. 'Post-Bourgeois Tattoo: Reflections on Skin Writing in Late Capitalist Societies'. *Visual Anthropology Review*, 7(2): 11–21.

Broadbridge, A. M., Maxwell, G. A. and Ogden, S. M. 2007. 'Experiences, Perceptions and Expectations of Retail Employment for Generation Y'. *Career Development International*, 12(6): 523–44.

Carmeli, A., Tishler, A. and Edmondson, A. C. 2012. 'CEO Relational Leadership and Strategic Decision Quality in Top Management Teams: The Role of Team Trust and Learning from Failure'. *Strategic Organization*, 10(1): 31–54.

Castells, M. 1996. *The Rise of the Network Society*. Cambridge, MA: Blackwell.

Charles, M. 2003. 'Deciphering Sex Segregation: Vertical and Horizontal Inequalities in Ten National Labor Markets'. *Acta Sociologica*, 46(4): 267–87.

Cheng, C. (ed.). 1996. *Masculinities in Organizations*. London: Sage.

Childress, M. D. and Braswell, R. 2006. 'Using Massively Multiplayer Online Role-Playing Games for Online Learning'. *Distance Education*, 27(2): 187–96.

Clance, P. R. and Imes, S. A. 1978. 'The Imposter Phenomenon in High Achieving Women: Dynamics and Therapeutic Intervention'. *Psychotherapy: Theory, Research & Practice*, 15(3): 241–7.

Coates, J. M., Gurnell, M. and Sarnyai, Z. 2010. 'From Molecule to Market: Steroid Hormones and Financial Risk-Taking'. *Philosophical Transactions of the Royal Society B: Biological Sciences*, 365(1538): 331–43.

Coates, J. M. and Herbert, J. 2008. 'Endogenous Steroids and Financial Risk Taking on a London Trading Floor'. *Proceedings of the National Academy of Sciences of the United States of America*, 105(16): 6167–72.

Cooper, M. 2000. 'Being the "Go-To Guy": Fatherhood, Masculinity, and the Organization of Work in Silicon Valley'. *Qualitative Sociology*, 23(4): 379–405.

Coppock, V., Haydon, D. and Richter, I. 1995. *The Illusions of 'Post-Feminism' – New Women, Old Myths*. London: Taylor and Francis.

Day, D. V. 2000. 'Leadership Development – A Review in Context'. *The Leadership Quarterly*, 11(4): 581–613.

Duncan, N. 2007. '"Feed-Forward": Improving Students' Use of Tutors' Comments'. *Assessment & Evaluation in Higher Education*, 32(3): 271–83.

Eagly, A. H. 2005. 'Achieving Relational Authenticity in Leadership: Does Gender Matter? *Leadership Quarterly*, 16(3): 459–74.

Eagly, A. H. and Karau, S. J. 1991. 'Gender and the Emergence of Leaders: A Meta-Analysis'. *Journal of Personality and Social Psychology*, 60(5): 685–710.

Edmondson, A. 1999. 'Psychological Safety and Learning Behavior in Work Teams'. *Administrative Science Quarterly*, 44(2): 350–83.

Edmondson, A. 2003. 'Speaking Up in the Operating Room: How Team Leaders Promote Learning in Interdisciplinary Action Teams'. *Journal of Management Studies*, 40(6): 1419–52.

Ehrenreich, B. and Hochschild, A. R. 2003. *Global Woman – Nannies, Maids, and Sex Workers in the New Economy*. New York: Metropolitan Books.

176

Ellemers, N., van den Heuvel, H., de Gilder, D., Maas, A. and Bovini, A. 2004. 'The Underrepresentation of Women in Science: Differential Commitment or the Queen Bee Syndrome?' *British Journal of Social Psychology*, 43(3): 315–38.

Entwistle, J. 2000. 'Fashioning the Career Woman: Power Dressing as a Strategy of Consumption'. In M. R. Andrews and M. M. Talbot (eds), *All the World and Her Husband*: 224–38. London Cassell.

Erickson, R. J. 1995. 'The Importance of Authenticity for Self and Society'. *Symbolic Interaction*, 18(2): 121–44.

Eurostat. 2011. 'Gender Pay Gap in Unadjusted Form'. http://epp.eurostat. ec.europa.eu/portal/page/portal/product_details/dataset?p_product_ code=TSDSC340.

Facebook. 2012. 'Timeline: Now Available Worldwide'. http://blog.facebook. com/blog.php?post=10150408488962131.

Farber, H. S. 2007. 'Is the Company Man an Anachronism? Trends in Long Term Employment in the U.S., 1973–2006'. http://arks.princeton.edu/ark:/88435/ dsp01ft848q61h.

Faulkner, W. 2000. 'Dualism, Hierarchies and Gender in Engineering'. *Social Studies of Science*, 30(5): 759–92.

Fausto-Sterling, A. 2000. *Sexing the Body: Gender Politics and the Construction of Sexuality*. New York: Basic Books.

Feldman, M. S. and Pentland, B. T. 2003. 'Reconceptualizing Organizational Routines as a Source of Flexibility and Change'. *Administrative Science Quarterly*, 48(1): 94–118.

Fenwick, T. 1998. 'Women Composing Selves, Seeking Authenticity: A Study of Women's Development in the Workplace'. *International Journal of Lifelong Education*, 17(3): 199–217.

Financial Times. 2012. 'Global MBA Rankings 2012'. http://rankings.ft.com/ businessschoolrankings/global-mba-rankings-2012.

Fine, C. 2010. *Delusions of Gender – The Real Science Behind Sex Differences*. London: Icon.

Fletcher, J. K. 2004. 'The Paradox of Postheroic Leadership: An Essay on Gender, Power, and Transformational Change'. *The Leadership Quarterly*, 15(5): 647–61.

Forret, M. L., Sullivan, S. E. and Mainiero, L. A. 2010. 'Gender Role Differences in Reactions to Unemployment: Exploring Psychological Mobility and Boundaryless Careers'. *Journal of Organizational Behavior*, 31(5): 647–66.

Fried-Buchalter, S. 1997. 'Fear of Success, Fear of Failure, and the Imposter Phenomenon among Male and Female Marketing Managers'. *Sex Roles*, 37(11–12): 847–59.

Gerson, K. 2002. 'Moral Dilemmas, Moral Strategies, and the Transformation of Gender Lessons from Two Generations of Work and Family Change'. *Gender & Society*, 16(1): 8–28.

Gherardi, S. and Poggio, B. 2001. 'Creating and Recreating Gender Order in Organizations'. *Journal of World Business*, 36(3): 245–59.

Ghoshal, S. 2005. 'Bad Management Theories are Destroying Good Management Practices'. *Academy of Management Learning & Education*, 4(1): 75–91.

Giddens, A. 1987. *Social Theory and Modern Sociology*. Cambridge: Polity Press.

Gill, R. 2006. *Gender and the Media*. Cambridge: Polity Press.

Goffee, R. and Jones, G. 2005. 'Managing Authenticity'. *Harvard Business Review*, 83(12): 86–94.

REFERENCES

Gratton, L., Kelan, E., Voigt, A., Walker, L. and Wolfram, H-J. 2007. 'Innovative Potential: Men and Women in Teams', The Lehman Brothers Centre for Women in Business, London Business School. http://www.elisabeth-kelan.net.

Gratton, L., Kelan, E. and Walker, L. 2007. 'Inspiring Women: Corporate Best Practice in Europe', The Lehman Brothers Centre for Women in Business, London Business School. http://www.elisabeth-kelan.net.

Groves, K. S. 2007. 'Integrating Leadership Development and Succession Planning Best Practices'. *Journal of Management Development*, 26(3): 236–60.

Groysberg, B. 2008. 'How Star Women Build Portable Skills'. *Harvard Business Review*, 86(2): 74–81.

Harris, M. 1976. 'History and Significance of the Emic/Etic Distinction'. *Annual Review of Anthropology*, 5(1976): 329–50.

Hausmann, R., Tyson, L. D. and Zahidi, S. 2011. 'The Global Gender Gap Report'. http://reports.weforum.org/global-gender-gap-2011/.

Healy, M. 2012. 'Millennials Might Not Be So Special After All, Study Finds', *USA Today*. http://www.usatoday.com/news/health/wellness/story/2012-03-15/Millennials-might-not-be-so-special-after-all-study-finds/53552744/1.

Heidegger, M. 1962. *Being and Time*. Oxford: Wiley-Blackwell.

Hewlett, S. A., Luce, C. B., Southwell, S. and Bernstein, L. 2007. 'Seduction and Risk: The Emergence of Extreme Jobs'. http://www.worklifepolicy.org/index.php/section/research_pubs.

Hill Collins, P. 2000. *Black Feminist Thought: Knowledge, Consciousness and the Politics of Empowerment*. London: Routledge.

Hollander, A. 1994. *Sex and Suits – The Evolution of Modern Dress*. Brinkworth: Claridge Press.

Hopkins, M. M., O'Neil, D. A., Passarelli, A. and Bilimoria, D. 2008. 'Women's Leadership Development Strategic Practices for Women and Organizations'. *Consulting Psychology Journal: Practice and Research*, 60(4): 348–65.

Hoque, K. and Kirkpatrick, I. 2003. 'Non-Standard Employment in the Management and Professional Workforce: Training, Consultation and Gender Implications'. *Work, Employment & Society*, 17(4): 667–89.

Hyde, J. S. 2005. 'The Gender Similarities Hypothesis'. *American Psychologist*, 60(6): 581–92.

Ibarra, H. 1992. 'Homophily and Differential Returns: Sex Differences in Network Structure and Access in an Advertising Firm'. *Administrative Science Quarterly*, 37(3): 422–47.

Ibarra, H. 2005. 'Identity Transitions: Possible Selves, Liminality and the Dynamics of Career Change', *INSEAD Working Paper Series*. Fontainbleau: INSEAD.

Ibarra, H., Carter, N. M. and Silva, C. 2010. 'Why Men Still Get More Promotions Than Women'. *Harvard Business Review*, 88(9): 80–5.

IBM and Seriosity. 2007. 'Virtual Worlds, Real Leaders: Online Games Put the Future of Business Leadership on Display'. http://www.seriosity.com/downloads/GIO_PDF_web.pdf.

Jarvis, H. and Pratt, A. C. 2006. 'Bringing It All Back Home: The Extensification and "Overflowing" of Work. The Case of San Francisco's New Media Households'. *GeoForum*, 37(3): 331–9.

Jayne, M. E. A. and Dipboye, R. L. 2004. 'Leveraging Diversity to Improve Business Performance: Research Findings and Recommendations for Organizations'. *Human Resource Management*, 43(4): 409–24.

Joshi, A., Dencker, J. C., Franz, G. and Martocchio, J. J. 2010. 'Unpacking Generational Identities in Organizations'. *Academy of Management Review*, 35(3): 392–414.

JWT. 2005. 'What Women Want – Addressing the Gender Imbalance in MBA Participation: Qualitative Summary Report'.

Kalev, A., Dobbin, F. and Kelly, E. 2006. 'Best Practices or Best Guesses? Assessing the Efficacy of Corporate Affirmative Action and Diversity'. *American Sociological Review*, 71(4): 589–617.

Kanter, R. M. 1977. *Men and Women of the Corporation*. New York: Basic Books.

Kanter, R. M. 1995. *World Class: Thriving Locally in the Global Economy*. London: Simon & Schuster.

Kee, H. J. 2006. 'Glass Ceiling or Sticky Floor? Exploring the Australian Gender Pay Gap'. *Economic Record*, 82(259): 408–27.

Kelan, E., Gratton, L., Mah, A. and Walker, L. 2009. 'The Reflexive Generation – Young Professionals' Perspectives on Work, Career and Gender'. http://www.elisabeth-kelan.net.

Kelan, E. K. 2008a. 'Bound by Stereotypes?' *Business Strategy Review*, 19(1): 4–7.

Kelan, E. K. 2008b. 'Emotions in a Rational Profession: The Gendering of Skills in ICT work'. *Gender, Work & Organization*, 15(1): 49–71.

Kelan, E. K. 2008c. 'Gender, Risk and Employment Insecurity: The Masculine Breadwinner Subtext'. *Human Relations*, 61(9): 1171–202.

Kelan, E. K. 2009a. 'Gender Fatigue – The Ideological Dilemma of Gender Neutrality and Discrimination in Organisations'. *Canadian Journal of Administrative Sciences*, 26(3): 197–210.

Kelan, E. K. 2009b. *Performing Gender at Work*. Basingstoke: Palgrave Macmillan.

Kelan, E. K. and Dunkley Jones, R. 2010. 'Gender and the MBA'. *Academy of Management Learning & Education*, 9(1): 26–43.

Kilian, C. M., Hukai, D. and McCarty, C. E. 2005. 'Building Diversity in the Pipeline to Corporate Leadership'. *Journal of Management Development*, 24(2): 155–68.

Kochan, T., Bezrukova, K., Ely, R., Jackson, S., Joshi, A., Jehn, K., Leonard, J., Levine, D. and Thomas, D. 2003. 'The Effects of Diversity on Business Performance: Report of the Diversity Research Network'. *Human Resource Management*, 42(1): 3–21.

Kolb, A. and Kolb, D. 2005. 'Learning Styles and Learning Spaces: Enhancing Experiential Learning in Higher Education'. *Academy of Management Learning & Education*, 4(2): 193–212.

Kolb, D. 1984. *Experiential Learning: Experience as the Source of Learning and Development*. Upper Saddle River, NJ: Prentice Hall.

Kossek, E. E. and Lambert, S. J. (eds). 2005. *Work and Life Integration: Organizational, Cultural, and Individual Perspectives*. Mahwah, NJ: Erlbaum.

Kotamraju, N. P. 2002. 'Keeping Up: Web Design Skill and the Reinvented Worker'. *Information, Communication & Society*, 5(1): 1–26.

Kray, L. J., Thompson, L. and Galinsky, A. 2001. 'Battle of the Sexes: Gender Stereotype Confirmation and Reactance in Negotiations. *Journal of Personality and Social Psychology*, 80(6): 942–58.

Levenson, A. R. 2010. 'Millennials and the World of Work: An Economist's Perspective'. *Journal of Business and Psychology*, 25(2): 257–64.

Lewis, J. 2001. 'The Decline of the Male Breadwinner Model: Implications for Work and Care'. *Social Politics*, 8(2): 152–69.

Liff, S. and Ward, K. 2001. 'Distorted Views through the Glass Ceiling: The Construction of Women's Understandings of Promotion and Senior Management Positions'. *Gender, Work & Organization*, 8(1): 19–36.

Lofland, J. and Lofland, L. H. 1984. *Analyzing Social Settings – A Guide to Qualitative Observation and Analysis* (Second Edition). Belmont, CA: Wadsworth.

Lorber, J. 1993. 'Believing is Seeing: Biology as Ideology'. *Gender and Society*, 7(4): 568–81.

Lynton, N. and Thogersen, K. H. 2010. 'Succeeding with Chinese Generation Y, Critical Eye'. http://www.nandanilynton.com/download/2010SucceedingwithGenY.pdf.

Maak, T. and Pless, N. M. 2006. 'Responsible Leadership in a Stakeholder Society – A Relational Perspective'. *Journal of Business Ethics*, 66(1): 99–115.

MacKenzie, D. and Wajcman, J. (eds). 1999. *The Social Shaping of Technology*. Buckingham: Open University Press.

Manning, A. and Petrongolo, B. 2008. 'The Part-Time Pay Penalty for Women in Britain'. *The Economic Journal*, 118(526): F28–F51.

Mavin, S. 2008. 'Queen Bees, Wannabees and Afraid to Bees: No More "Best Enemies" for Women in Management?' *British Journal of Management*, 19(S1): S75–S84.

McCall, L. 2001. *Complex Inequalities: Gender, Class and Race in the New Economy*. London: Routledge.

McCarty, P. A. 1986. 'Effects of Feedback on the Self-Confidence of Men and Women'. *Academy of Management Journal*, 29(4): 840–7.

McRobbie, A. 2008. *The Aftermath of Feminism: Gender, Culture and Social Change*. London: Sage.

Mielach, D. 2012. 'Gen Y Seeks Work-Life Balance Above All Else', *Fox Business*. http://smallbusiness.foxbusiness.com/legal-hr/2012/03/30/gen-y-seeks-work-life-balance-above-all-else/.

Miller, D. L. and Karakowsky, L. 2005. 'Gender Influences as an Impediment to Knowledge Sharing: When Men and Women Fail to Seek Peer Feedback'. *The Journal of Psychology: Interdisciplinary and Applied*, 139(2): 101–18.

Moore, R. L. 2005. 'Generation Ku: Individualism and China's Millennial Youth. *Ethnology*, 44(4): 357–76.

Nielsen. 2009. 'The State of the Video Gamer'. http://blog.nielsen.com/nielsen-wire/wp-content/uploads/2009/04/stateofgamer_040609_fnl1.pdf.

OECD. 2012. 'Women and Men in OECD Countries'. http://www.oecd.org/dataoecd/44/52/37962502.pdf.

Opportunity Now. 2011. 'Global Award – American Express – Becoming a Gender Intelligent Workplace'. http://www.bitcdiversity.org.uk/awards/on_awards_2011/on_awards_case_studies_2011/global/american_express.html.

Opportunity Now. 2012. 'The Inclusive Culture Award – PwC'. http://www.bitcdiversity.org.uk/awards/on_awards_2012/inclusive_culture/the_inclusive_2.html.

Özbilgin, M. F., Beauregard, T. A., Tatli, A. and Bell, M. P. 2011. 'Work-Life, Diversity and Intersectionality: A Critical Review and Research Agenda'. *International Journal of Management Reviews*, 13(2): 177–98.

Parsons, T. and Bales, R. 1956. *Family and Socialization and Interaction Process*. London: Routledge.

Patten, E. and Parker, K. 2012. 'A Gender Reversal on Career Aspirations – Young Women Now Top Young Men in Valuing a High-Paying Career', Pew Social & Demographic Trends. http://www.pewsocialtrends.org/files/2012/04/Women-in-the-Workplace.pdf.

Phipps, A. 2006. '"I Can't Do With Whinging Women!" Feminism and the Habitus of "Women in Science" Activists'. *Women's Studies International Forum*, 29(2): 125–35.

Pongratz, H. J. and Voß, G. G. 2003. 'From Employee to "Entreployee": Towards a "Self-Entrepreneurial" Work Force?' *Concepts and Transformation*, 8(3): 239–54.

Porter, M. and Kramer, M. 2011. 'Creating Shared Value'. *Harvard Business Review*, 89(1/2): 62–77.

Quimby, J. L. and DeSantis, A. M. 2006. 'The Influence of Role Models on Women's Career Choices'. *Career Development Quarterly*, 54(4): 297–306.

Ragins, B. and Cotton, J. 1999. 'Mentor Functions and Outcomes: A Comparison of Men and Women in Formal and Informal Mentoring Relationships'. *Journal of Applied Psychology*, 84(4): 529–50.

Reeskens, T. and van Oorschot, W. (2012) 'Those who are in the gutter look at the stars? Explaining Perceptions of Labour Market Opportunities among European Young Adults'. *Work, Employment Society*, 26(3): 379–95.

Reeves, B. and Malone, T. 2007. 'Leadership in Games and at Work: Implications for the Enterprise of Massively Multiplayer Online Role-playing Games'. http://www.seriosity.com/downloads/Leadership_In_Games_Seriosity_and_IBM.pdf.

Robbins, A. and Wilner, A. 2001. *Quarterlife Crisis: The Unique Challenges of Life in Your Twenties*. New York: Jeremy P Tarcher.

Roberson, L., Deitch, E. A., Brief, A. P. and Block, C. J. 2003. 'Stereotype Threat and Feedback Seeking in the Workplace'. *Journal of Vocational Behavior*, 62(1): 176–88.

Roberson, L. and Kulik, C. 2007. 'Stereotype Threat at Work'. *Academy of Management Perspectives*, 21(2): 24–40.

Ryan, M. K. and Haslam, S. A. 2005. 'The Glass Cliff: Evidence that Women are Over-Represented in Precarious Leadership Positions'. *British Journal of Management*, 16: 81–90.

Sandell, R. 1993. 'Envy and Admiration'. *International Journal of Psychoanalysis*, 74(6): 1213–22.

Scharff, C. 2011a. 'Disarticulating Feminism: Individualization, Neoliberalism and the Othering of Muslim Women'. *European Journal of Women's Studies*, 18(2): 119–34.

Scharff, C. 2011b. '"It is a Colour Thing and a Status Thing, rather than a Gender Thing": Negotiating Difference in Talk about Feminism'. *Feminism & Psychology*, 21(4): 458–76.

Scharff, C. 2011c. 'Young Women's Negotiations of Heterosexual Conventions: Theorizing Sexuality in Constructions of "the Feminist"'. *Sociology*, 44(5): 827–42.

Scharff, C. 2012. *Repudiating Feminism*. Farnham: Ashgate.

Schein, E. H. 2010. *Organizational Culture and Leadership*. San Francisco: Jossey Bass.

Schein, V. E., Mueller, R., Lituchy, T. and Liu, J. 1996. 'Think Manager – Think Male: A Global Phenomenon?' *Journal of Organizational Behavior*, 17(1): 33–41.

Sennett, R. 1998. *The Corrosion of Character: The Personal Consequences of Work in the New Capitalism*. New York: Norton.

Shamir, B. and Eilam, G. 2005. '"What's Your Story?" A Life-Stories Approach to Authentic Leadership Development'. *The Leadership Quarterly*, 16(3): 395–417.

Simmons. 2012. The Simmons MBA. http://www.simmons.edu/som/programs/mba/.

Sinclair, A. 1995. 'Sex and the MBA'. *Organization*, 2(2): 295–317.

Smith, N., Smith, V. and Verne, M. 2010. 'The Gender Pay Gap in Top Corporate Jobs in Denmark: Glass Ceilings, Sticky Floors or Both?' *International Journal of Manpower*, 32(2): 156–77.

Smithson, J. and Stokoe, E. H. 2005. 'Discourses of Work-Life Balance: Negotiating "Genderblind" Terms in Organizations'. *Gender, Work and Organization*, 12(2): 147–68.

Sparrowe, R. T. 2005. 'Authentic Leadership and the Narrative Self'. *The Leadership Quarterly*, 16(3): 419–39.

Strauss, W. and Howe, N. 1991. *Generations: The History of America's Future, 1584 to 2069*. New York: William Morrow and Company.

Trice, H. M. and Beyer, J. M. 1984. 'Studying Organizational Cultures through Rites and Ceremonials'. *The Academy of Management Review*, 9(4): 653–69.

Turner, V. 1969. *The Ritual Process: Structure and Anti-Structure*. New York: Aldine de Gruyter.

Twenge, J. M. 1997. 'Changes in Masculine and Feminine Traits Over Time: A Meta-Analysis'. *Sex Roles*, 36(5–6): 305–25.

Twenge, J. M. 2009. 'Status and Gender: The Paradox of Progress in an Age of Narcissism'. *Sex Roles*, 61(5–6): 338–40.

Twenge, J. M. 2010. 'A Review of the Empirical Evidence on Generational Differences in Work Attitudes'. *Journal of Business and Psychology*, 25(2): 201–10.

Twenge, J. M. and Campbell, S. M. 2008. 'Generational Differences in Psychological Traits and their Impact on the Workplace'. *Journal of Managerial Psychology*, 23(8): 862–77.

Twenge, J. M., Campbell, W. K. and Freeman, E. C. 2012. 'Generational Differences in Young Adults' Life Goals – Concern for Others, and Civic Orientation, 1966–2009'. *Journal of Personality and Social Psychology*, 102(5): 1045–62.

Twenge, J. M., Campbell, S. M., Hoffman, B. J. and Lance, C. E. 2010. 'Generational Differences in Work Values: Leisure and Extrinsic Values Increasing, Social and Intrinsic Values Decreasing'. *Journal of Management*, 36(5): 1117–42.

Twitaholic. 2012. 'The Twitaholic.com Top 100 Twitterholics based on Followers'. http://twitaholic.com/top100/followers/.

Van Gennep, A. 1960. *The Rites of Passage* (M. B. Vizedom and G. L. Caffee, Trans.). London: Routledge and Kegan Paul.

Vinnicombe, S. and Singh, V. 2003. 'Women-Only Management Training: An Essential Part of Women's Leadership Development?' *Journal of Change Management*, 3(4): 294–306.

Wajcman, J. 1998. *Managing Like a Man*. Oxford: Blackwell.

Walter, N. 1998. *The New Feminism*. London: Little Brown and Company.

Weber, M. 1934/1993. *Die Protestantische Ethik und der 'Geist' des Kapitalismus*. Bodenheim: Neue Wissenschaftliche Bibliothek.

Westen, D. 1999. 'The Scientific Status of Unconscious Processes: Is Freud Really Dead?' *Journal of the American Psychoanalytic Association*, 47(4): 1061–106.

Woodfield, R. 2000. *Women, Work and Computing*. Cambridge: Cambridge University Press.

Yee, N. 2006. 'The Labor of Fun – How Video Games Blur the Boundaries of Work and Play'. *Games and Culture*, 1(1): 68–71.

Zickuhr, K. 2010. 'Generations 2010', Pew Internet & American Life Project. http://www.pewinternet.org/~/media//Files/Reports/2010/PIP_Generations_and_Tech10.pdf.

Zuo, J. 1997. 'The Effect of Men's Breadwinner Status on their Changing Gender Beliefs'. *Sex Roles*, 37(9–10): 799–816.

Index